12/06

D0538433

Jane Yolen

WHO WROTE THAT?

Jane Yolen

Carolyn Carpan

Foreword by
Kyle Zimmer

CHELSEA HOUSE
PUBLISHERS
A Haights Cross Communications Company ®
Philadelphia

CHELSEA HOUSE PUBLISHERS

VP, New Product Development Sally Cheney
Director of Production Kim Shinners
Creative Manager Takeshi Takahashi
Manufacturing Manager Diann Grasse

Staff for JANE YOLEN

Executive Editor Matt Uhler
Editorial Assistant Sarah Sharpless
Production Editor Noelle Nardone
Photo Editor Sarah Bloom
Interior and Cover Designer Keith Trego
Layout 21st Century Publishing and Communications, Inc.

First Printing

1 3 5 7 9 8 6 4 2

Library of Congress Cataloging-in-Publication Data applied

Carpan, Carolyn.
  Jane Yolen/Carolyn Carpan.
    p. cm.—(Who wrote that?)
  Includes bibliographical references and index.
  ISBN 0-7910-8660-7
  1. Yolen, Jane—Juvenile literature. 2. Authors, American—20th century—
Biography—Juvenile literature. 3. Children's literature—Authorship—Juvenile
literature. I. Title. II. Series.
PS3575.O43Z63 2005
813'.54—dc22
                                                        2005007828

All links and Web addresses were checked and verified to be correct at the time
of publication. Because of the dynamic nature of the Web, some addresses
and links may have changed since publication and may no longer be valid.

Table of Contents

FOREWORD BY
KYLE ZIMMER
PRESIDENT, FIRST BOOK

HUMANITY IS POWERED by stories. From our earliest days as thinking beings, we employed every available tool to tell each other stories. We danced, drew pictures on the walls of our caves, spoke, and sang. All of this extraordinary effort was designed to entertain, recount the news of the day, explain natural occurrences—and then gradually to build religious and cultural traditions and establish the common bonds and continuity that eventually formed civilizations. Stories are the most powerful force in the universe; they are the primary element that has distinguished our evolutionary path.

Our love of the story has not diminished with time. Enormous segments of societies are devoted to the art of storytelling. Book sales in the United States alone topped $26 billion last year; movie studios spend fortunes to create and promote stories; and the news industry is more pervasive in its presence than ever before.

There is no mystery to our fascination. Great stories are magic. They can introduce us to new cultures, or remind us of the nobility and failures of our own, inspire us to greatness or scare us to death; but above all, stories provide human insight on a level that is unavailable through any other source. In fact, stories connect each of us to the rest of humanity not just in our own time, but also throughout history.

This special magic of books is the greatest treasure that we can hand down from generation to generation. In fact, that spark in a child that comes from books became the motivation for the creation of my organization, First Book, a national literacy program with a simple mission: to provide new books to the most disadvantaged children. At present, First Book has been at work in hundreds of communities for over a decade. Every year children in need receive millions of books through our organization and millions more are provided through dedicated literacy institutions across the United States and around the world. In addition, groups of people dedicate themselves tirelessly to working with children to share reading and stories in every imaginable setting from schools to the streets. Of course, this Herculean effort serves many important goals. Literacy translates to productivity and employability in life and many other valid and even essential elements. But at the heart of this movement are people who love stories, love to read, and want desperately to ensure that no one misses the wonderful possibilities that reading provides.

When thinking about the importance of books, there is an overwhelming urge to cite the literary devotion of great minds. Some have written of the magnitude of the importance of literature. Amy Lowell, an American poet, captured the concept when she said, "Books are more than books. They are the life, the very heart and core of ages past, the reason why men lived and worked and died, the essence and quintessence of their lives." Others have spoken of their personal obsession with books, as in Thomas Jefferson's simple statement, "I live for books." But more compelling, perhaps, is the almost instinctive excitement in children for books and stories.

Throughout my years at First Book, I have heard truly extraordinary stories about the power of books in the lives of children. In one case, a homeless child, who had been bounced from one location to another, later resurfaced— and the only possession that he had fought to keep was the book he was given as part of a First Book distribution months earlier. More recently, I met a child who, upon receiving the book he wanted, flashed a big smile and said, "This is my big chance!" These snapshots reveal the true power of books and stories to give hope and change lives.

As these children grow up and continue to develop their love of reading, they will owe a profound debt to those volunteers who reached out to them—a debt that they may repay by reaching out to spark the next generation of readers. But there is a greater debt owed by all of us— a debt to the storytellers, the authors, who have bound us together, inspired our leaders, fueled our civilizations, and helped us put our children to sleep with their heads full of images and ideas.

WHO WROTE THAT? is a series of books dedicated to introducing us to a few of these incredible individuals. While we have almost always honored stories, we have not uniformly honored storytellers. In fact, some of the most important authors have toiled in complete obscurity throughout their lives or have been openly persecuted for the uncomfortable truths that they have laid before us. When confronted with the magnitude of their written work or perhaps the daily grind of our own, we can forget that writers are people. They struggle through the same daily indignities and dental appointments, and they experience the intense joy and bottomless despair that many of us do. Yet somehow they rise above it all to deliver a powerful thread that connects us all. It is a rare honor to have the opportunity that these books provide to share the lives of these extraordinary people. Enjoy.

Hans Christian Andersen (1805–1875), pictured here, was a Danish author famous for writing fairy tales, including "Princess and the Pea," "Ugly Duckling," and "Emperor's New Clothes." Andersen has been a source and inspiration for Jane Yolen's writing.

An Ordinary Life

LIKE MANY YOUNG girls, when she was growing up Jane Yolen dreamed of becoming a ballerina. She loved to dance. When the Yolen family lived in New York City, Yolen took dance lessons at the American School of Ballet. The famous choreographer (creator of dances) George Balanchine was her teacher. Yolen has said of that time, "I was one of thousands of little girls who wanted to become ballerinas, but I was luckier than most. I got to train at Balanchine's School of American Ballet. We students were allowed to watch rehearsals, but only if we were absolutely quiet and did not move out of the room the entire time—not even to get something to eat or to go to the bathroom. Once out, you were not allowed back in!"[1]

But as Yolen grew up, she realized with disappointment that she didn't have the body to become a professional ballerina. Although Yolen continued to take dance lessons, she knew she would never end up as a famous ballerina like her idol, Maria Tallchief.

However, Yolen displayed many other talents from a very young age. She liked to sing and play the piano. She also enjoyed writing stories, poems, and songs. Writing wasn't something anyone told her she should do. She wrote for fun. When Yolen was a child she thought a lot about what she wanted to be when she grew up. She considered becoming a ballerina or possibly a lawyer. She also wanted to own a horse ranch. Since Yolen enjoyed writing so much, it was natural for her to think about becoming a professional writer. By the time she graduated from college, Yolen had decided to pursue a writing career.

Today Jane Yolen is a world-renowned author of children's books. She is a versatile and prolific writer, with more than 250 books to her name. Her books have been translated into many different languages. Yolen writes picture books, poetry, and nonfiction books for young readers. She also writes many different genres of fiction, including fantasy, science fiction, historical fiction, mysteries, and even romance stories. She also composes music and has published a number of songbooks. Yolen also writes fantasy novels and poetry for adults.

Yolen is best known for her Caldecott Medal-winning picture book *Owl Moon*, her graphic Holocaust story *The Devil's Arithmetic*, and her best-selling picture book *How Do Dinosaurs Say Good Night?* She is also well known for her original fairy tales, such as *The Emperor and the Kite*,

The Girl Who Loved the Wind, *The Girl Who Cried Flowers and Other Tales*, *The Boy Who Had Wings*, *The Seeing Stick*, *Good Griselle*, *The Girl in the Golden Bower*, and *Dove Isabeau*. Yolen hopes she will be remembered for her original fairy tales.

Prominent themes in Yolen's writing include religion, pacificism, music, dancing, family, and friendship. She also writes about serious subjects such as death, grief, multiculturalism, and the need to please one's parents. Another trend displayed in Yolen's work is her choice to have her main characters be independent women. These women are often portrayed in nontraditional roles. Yolen has written many stories based on the legends about King Arthur as well as other popular myths. While she enjoys writing her own original fairy tales, she also writes retellings of popular fairy tales. Fantastic beings often appear in her books: dragons, ghosts, witches, unicorns, mermaids, selchies (creatures who are human on land and seals in water), and wizards. Yolen is particularly fond of dragons.

Yolen's writing talent has helped her to become a famous author, allowing her to leave behind her dreams of becoming a famous ballerina. In fact, when Yolen's children were growing up, they jokingly referred to her as a "Famous Author"

Did you know...

Jane Yolen loves dragons. She often writes stories about dragons. Yolen displays her collection of model dragons in her office. She also has a collection of unicorns, selchies, wizards, and mermaids. Yolen claims she once saw a merman (male mermaid) in Greenwich, England. She even has a photo of it!

Above is a drawing of Aesop the reputed author of Aesop's Fables, a collection of stories with animals as main characters. Because of her interest in fantastic creatures in her own stories, Jane Yolen has been referred to as a "modern equivalent of Aesop."

whenever she had to give a speech or go to a conference. All jokes aside, Yolen truly has reached a pinnacle of achievement and fame during her writing career. She has been dubbed "America's Hans Christian Andersen" by *Newsweek* magazine, and the *The New York Times Book Review* has referred to her as "a modern equivalent of Aesop."[2] Of course, Yolen is honored by the awards and the recognition she receives for her work, but she doesn't think about her fame very often because she is usually too busy working on her latest books and sharing her life with family and friends.

If you ask Yolen, she will tell you her life has been very ordinary. "It used to bother me that I had lived such an ordinary life: born in New York City, public school education, an uneventful childhood with no major traumas, college that was smooth but unexciting, marriage to the same man for over thirty-five years, and three children."[3] But Yolen has actually had many exciting adventures. She once rescued her father from Long Island Sound when his large kite dragged him into the water. Yolen learned to dance the twist in a bar alongside New York City's finest garbagemen. And she hiked up Mount Pelion in Greece when she was more than seven months pregnant. She also claims she saw a merman (male mermaid) in Greenwich, England. Above all, Yolen has published hundreds of books, won many awards, and touched people around the world with her writing. While Yolen's life may seem fairly ordinary, her 40-year writing career has been extraordinary. She is a writer, editor, storyteller, poet, teacher, singer, music composer, friend, wife, mother, and grandmother. "I wear a lot of hats," Yolen once said in a video about her work.[4] Her sense of humor helps her find balance in her life. While she absolutely loves writing, Yolen also treasures her latest role as grandmother to Glendon, Maddison, Alison, David, Caroline, and Amelia.

Jane Yolen grew up in New York City in the 1940s. She had a wide variety of interests. She enjoyed reading, writing, music, and ballet dancing. Here we see a picture taken in the 1940s of Times Square in New York City.

2

From "Just Plain Jane" to a "Gold Star Star"

JANE HYATT YOLEN was born on February 11, 1939, at Beth Israel Hospital in New York City to William Hyatt Yolen and Isabelle Berlin Yolen. The Yolens were a family of Jewish merchants, social workers, and storytellers. Her great-grandfather Yolen was a respected storyteller in a small Ukrainian village. As a boy, her father Will Yolen lived with his family in Ukraine. The Yolens immigrated to the United States when Will was 4 years old. Will met Isabelle Berlin when he was working as a journalist in New York City. Isabelle Berlin came from an intellectual family who thought education was very

17

important. Isabelle was a social worker when she met Will Yolen. Will and Isabelle were secretly married at City Hall. They didn't tell their families that they had been married. Later they married again in a religious ceremony. This time their families were invited to attend the wedding. Will and Isabelle always thought of their second wedding as their "real" wedding. They celebrated their anniversary on that second date, February 23, 1934.

Isabelle worked as a social worker until her daughter was born. Then she stayed home to raise Yolen. Isabelle also did volunteer work. In her spare time, she wrote stories and crossword puzzles. While her stories were never published, her crossword puzzles often were. Isabelle loved to read mystery stories, too. Will was a published author, editor, and journalist. He wrote plays, radio scripts, and magazine articles. (He sometimes used the pen name Phillips H. Lord.) Will was also a world champion kite flier; he helped make kiting a popular sport in the 1950s. *Life* magazine once published a picture of Will flying a kite. He is in the *Guinness Book of World Records* for keeping a kite in the air for 179 hours. Will also enjoyed playing his guitar and singing songs.

In 1940, the Yolens moved to California. Will worked as a publicist at Warner Brothers movie studios. He worked on movies such as *Knute Rockne All American* (1940), which starred a young Ronald Reagan. Reagan went on to become the governor of California and then the president of the United States in 1980. The Yolens lived next door to Walter Brennan, star of Western movies and the television show *The Real McCoys*. The Yolens returned to New York City in 1942. On November 4, 1942, Isabelle gave birth to a baby boy who they named Steven Hyatt Yolen.

In 1944, Will Yolen went to England to serve as a Second Lieutenant in World War II. He worked as the head of the secret European radio broadcasting service called ABSIE. Four-year-old Yolen, her mother, and baby brother Steven moved to Chesapeake Bay, Virginia, to live with Isabelle's parents. Yolen clearly remembers the two-and-a-half years she lived with Grandma Fanny and Grandpa Dan Berlin. "The reason I recall that time so vividly was that my grandfather, whom I adored, died of a sudden and unexpected heart attack while we were there," Yolen wrote in an autobiographical essay.[5]

Grandma Fanny was very sad after her husband died. She cried often. Yolen recalled, "After my grandfather died, the house seemed haunted and cold."[6] Yolen was afraid to go into her grandmother's bedroom. Instead, she and Steven played in a long closet that joined their bedroom to Grandma Fanny's room. "Every night after Grandpa's death I closed the closet door and shoved a chair up under the handle," Yolen remembered.[7] Yolen has happy memories of living with her grandmother, too. She stated, "What I recall most is sitting on top of the table, my chubby little legs tucked under me, helping chop apples in a big wooden bowl for Grandma's applesauce."[8]

Yolen frequently played with her cousins on her mother's side. She and her cousin Michael Garrick, who was a year older than Yolen, often got into trouble. "We would go down to the Bay and wade in it though we had been warned again and again not to," Yolen wrote.[9] Their parents always knew they had been wading in the Bay. Fuel tankers and war ships often docked in Chesapeake Bay, leaving fuel oil in the water. The fuel oil stuck to the children's legs when they got out of the water. One day Yolen and Michael decided to go swimming in the Bay. When Grandma Fanny discovered what they had done, they were punished with spankings and a long soak in the bathtub.

Despite the fun she had playing with her cousins, Yolen believed she was a failure as a Southerner. "[A]ll the other girls on the block had names like 'Frances Bird' and 'Mary Alice.' I was just plain Jane," she recalled.[10] Yolen would later write about her time spent living in the south in a picture book titled *Miz Berlin Walks*. She remembered how Grandma Fanny loved to walk around the neighborhood. Another picture book, *All Those Secrets of the World*, recounts her reactions and those of her baby brother Steven to their father's departure for England, and his return from World War II two years later. Will left the war after he was injured during a bombing. "There were no big ships or waving flags, just a stranger in brown with his arm in a sling unfolding himself from a cab," Yolen wrote of her father's return.[11] "He told me that he'd won the war single-handedly, and I believed him," she said.[12]

The Yolen family moved back to New York City in 1945. By then Yolen had begun writing. Before she started school, she wrote the following poem:

Bus, bus, wait for us.
We are going to school, and we know the rule.
We were going to the zoo, but the teacher got sick. Boo-hoo.
So, instead we went to pick berries, but could only find cherries.
The end.[13]

"That is truly awful!" she admitted in an interview. "But I was in preschool, and I could rhyme."[14] Yolen's mother loved the poem and kept it for years. By the second grade, Yolen had gone to half a dozen schools. Her mother wanted to find the best school for her. Yolen remembered, "One time we even lied about where we lived to get into a better school, but I was too young to remember the pretend address, and so was found out."[15] She had to leave that school.

When she was young, Yolen enjoyed reading. After her first-grade teacher at Public School (PS) 93 discovered Yolen had read the semester's reading book overnight, she was moved to the second grade. Some of Yolen's favorite books were *Little Women* by Louisa May Alcott, *Charlotte's Web* by E.B. White, *The Secret Garden* by Frances Hodgson Burnett, and *The Wind in the Willows* by Kenneth Grahame. She also liked *Kidnapped* and *Treasure Island* by Robert Louis Stevenson. But Yolen loved reading folktales and fairy tales most of all. She often read sitting in a window seat, looking out over New York's Central Park.

When Yolen wasn't busy reading, she spent time with her friend Diane Sheffield. Diane lived in the apartment across the hall. Yolen recalled, "We were both tomboys, and we played rough-and-tumble games in the grass and rocks of Central Park."[16] Yolen especially liked the stories about King Arthur. Yolen, Diane, and her brother Steven would often pretend to be characters from the King Arthur stories. Diane and Steven played the evil characters, while Yolen chose to play the heroes.

Did you know...

When Jane Yolen was in junior high school, she studied ballet at Balanchine's American School of Ballet in New York City. One day, the famous ballerina Maria Tallchief taught Yolen's ballet class. After the class, she was delighted when the famous teacher hung her practice tutu on Yolen's locker.

At school, Yolen's writing talents began to show. Her teachers encouraged her to write. In second grade, the teacher gave Yolen an assignment to create her own world. "I drew on a big piece of posterboard, a big candy cane island. And I wrote a song that went with it. . . . The words go like this: *Where is the candy cane island? Where in the world can it be? Right across dreamland, across the canal, just come and follow me. There is Santa Claus's summer home, and Jack Frost lives there, too,*" Yolen said in an interview.[17]

Amazingly, Yolen wrote the musical for her second-grade class, including the words and the music. All the students played vegetables. Yolen was the lead carrot. The play ended with the students forming a big salad. Yolen's teachers recognized her creativity with gold stars. "I won gold stars and gold stars and more gold stars. I was the gold star star. And I was also pretty impossibly full of myself," Yolen admitted.[18]

In sixth grade, Yolen was accepted to Hunter Junior High School, an all-girls school for gifted students. She expected to be a star at Hunter, too. Instead, she realized she was an average student: "Then I tested and got into Hunter Junior High School and discovered that there were a lot of gold star girls all over the city. What a shock! I had to work hard just to stay in the middle of the class."[19] Yolen decided to concentrate on developing other talents besides writing. Music became an important part of her life. She sang, played the piano, and wrote songs. Yolen also starred as Hansel in the school musical *Hansel and Gretel*. Her father, who played guitar and sang, taught Yolen some folk songs. She discovered she loved folk songs and quickly learned many on her own.

Although she wasn't destined to be a great dancer, Yolen studied ballet dancing at Balanchine's American School

This is an illustration from Louisa May Alcott's Little Women, *one of Jane Yolen's favorite books as a girl.*

of Ballet. One day, the famous ballerina Maria Tallchief taught her ballet class. After the class, she was thrilled when the famous teacher hung her practice tutu on Yolen's locker. Eventually, Yolen gave up dancing in order to concentrate on her true gifts—writing stories and music. Yolen wrote, "[I]t became increasingly clear that my body type harkened back to the Yolens—short, squat, and while athletic and graceful, not . . . anorexic like a Balanchine dancer." [20]

Yolen continued to write stories while attending junior high school at Hunter. In the eighth grade, she wrote her first two books. She wrote a nonfiction book about pirates and she created a 17-page adventure story. The story included a trip to the West in a covered wagon, snakes, locusts, and a prairie fire. Yolen also spent time with her friend Anne Rosenwasser, who she knew from ballet class and school. Together they created a game in which they pretended Anne was a prima ballerina and Yolen was a top choreographer. The girls would create ballets and stories, which would always include famous boyfriends and plenty of exciting drama.

Although Yolen's family was Jewish, they didn't actively practice their religion. When she was 13 years old, the Yolens decided to join a synagogue so that Yolen could learn about her heritage and the Jewish religion. Yolen became the first girl to read from the Torah in the history of the family's temple. She also became the head of the temple youth group.

During the summers when she was 12 and 13 years old, Yolen attended a Quaker summer camp in Vermont called Indianbrook. Quakers are a Christian group founded in England in the mid-seventeenth century. Yolen learned about the Quaker's belief in pacifism, the peaceful opposition to war and violence; swimming; the arts of storytelling and planting a garden; the cleaning out of horse stalls; and how to kiss. At the end of Yolen's second summer at Indianbrook in 1952, she was told that her family had moved to Westport, Connecticut. Yolen and her brother Steven were sad because they weren't allowed to return to New York to say good-bye to friends and familiar places. Instead, their Uncle Harry and Aunt Isabelle picked them up at camp and drove them to Connecticut to join their parents in their new home.

Yolen was particularly disappointed about the family's sudden and unexpected move for several reasons. She had been accepted by the High School of Music and Art, where she wanted to study music. Yolen's first boyfriend, whom she had begun to date that summer at camp, lived in New York. And Yolen knew she would miss her friend Anne Rosenwasser.

In Westport, Yolen attended Bedford Junior High School and Staples High School. Her high school life became very busy. She was involved in the Jewish youth group, the school newspaper, the school literary magazine, and several singing groups. She was also the vice president of the Spanish and Latin clubs. Although Yolen was the shortest student on the girls' basketball team, she was chosen to be captain of the team. Yolen continued to study dance and piano. She even took horseback-riding lessons. During her spare time, she wrote poetry. Her poem "Death, You Do Not Frighten Me" won a Scholastic Writing Award.[21]

Yolen found new friends in Westport. Her first friend, Stella Colandrea, was Catholic. While Yolen was familiar with the Jewish and Quaker religions, she was fascinated when Stella introduced her to Catholicism. Yolen attended church services and Christmas Midnight Mass with the

Colandrea family. "It was because of Stella's influence that I became enamored of different religions," Yolen acknowledged.[22] Yolen continues to be fascinated with religious rituals. Her knowledge of Judaism, Catholicism, and Quakerism would later emerge in her fantasy stories. When they weren't at school or in church, Yolen and Stella wrote naughty poems about boys in their class. They often did their homework together outside on the porch roof of the Colandrea home.

Despite having several good friends, Yolen found that she was only somewhat popular in high school. She split her time between two separate groups of friends: the intellectuals and the fast social crowd. "I developed a wisecracking, cynical patter and an ability to tell funny stories which was, I think, why I was kept around," Yolen stated in an autobiographical essay.[23] Yolen had a reputation as a good girl. She wanted to please her parents and still remembers her mother's expectations clearly: "She expected good grades of me, hoped I might enjoy a bit of popularity but not too much, desired college as a definite, and sex as a definite no-no till marriage."[24] When Yolen was 16 she hosted a small party that quickly got out of control. "It was crashed by the entire (winning) Staples High School football team . . . Some boys sneaked in drinks and what had started as a quiet party turned into a rout," Yolen remembered.[25] Yolen's father didn't speak to her for a week. Her mother, on the other hand, took care of her intoxicated boyfriend and helped her clean up after the party.

Yolen spent a lot of time with her cousin-in-law Honey Knopp. Honey was a pacifist and a peace activist. Honey held hootenannies (folk musical parties) at her house. "I adored Honey and her husband Burt, and their home became my haven," Yolen said in an autobiographical essay.[26] Honey gave Yolen her first copy of Quaker founder George Fox's *Journal*. (Yolen would later write a biography about George Fox titled *Friend: The Story of George Fox and the Quakers*.) Yolen shared her serious poetry only with Honey. She kept her poetic side hidden from her friends at school; she didn't count the poems she wrote with Stella as real poetry. "This was in the mid-1950s, when to be interested in such things branded one an outsider, a beatnik, a left winger," Yolen stated.[27] She didn't want to be labeled a misfit at school.

Unfortunately, Yolen's wardrobe already made her feel like something of an outcast. Her mother insisted on making all of Yolen's clothing, but Isabelle was not very good at sewing. "The blouses she made had sleeves that were never set in properly; the skirts were style-less, with flawed waistbands. I never got to pick out the materials and I hated her every choice," Yolen recalled.[28] Yolen refused to let her mother sew her prom dress. Instead, Yolen picked out her dress at a secondhand clothing store that Isabelle ran for the Staples High School Parent Teacher Association.

When Yolen was a senior in high school, she was named "The Perfect Senior" for her singing voice. She graduated from Staples High School in 1956, noting, "I graduated seventh in my class. If I had worked hard, I might have gotten into my first choice college—Radcliffe. As it was, I was accepted at Oberlin, Wellesley, and Smith. I chose Smith."[29]

During the summer of 1956, Yolen worked at a camp run by the American Friends (Quaker) Service Committee in Yellow Springs, Ohio. While there, Yolen helped build an outdoor education center for the children of migrant workers. She also worked in a daycare center. Yolen remembered,

"I worked harder than I had ever worked before—for no pay."[30]

In the fall of 1956, Yolen enrolled at Smith College. "I discovered (again) that all the gold star girls around America were there," she said.[31] She studied English, Russian literature, religion, history, sociology, and geology. Yolen found there were many wonderful teachers at Smith who encouraged her to write. Although one of the determining factors in her decision to attend Smith was because the college had a strong music program, she only sang in the Smith College choirs for one year. Instead, Yolen became involved in folk singing and musical theatre. She also ran many campus organizations and wrote lots of poetry. Her poems were published in Smith College's *Grecourt Review*, *Poetry Digest*, and several other small magazines. Yolen won the poetry prize during her senior year at Smith College.

During the summers she was in college, Yolen worked at several different kinds of jobs. In the summer of 1957, she worked as a reporter for the *Bridgeport Sunday Herald*. When her first article was published in the newspaper, her byline mistakenly read "by Joan Yolen." "I did not take it as a sign," she recalled. "But I quickly learned that I was not a tough reporter when the editor assigned me to write an article on welfare recipients. I came back after the interviews and cried at my desk. I wanted to help those people, not write about them."[32] The following summer, Yolen worked as a camp counselor in New Jersey. Her parents had refused her request for permission to work with the Quakers that summer. Yolen wanted to work with sick Eskimo in Alaska. But her parents were afraid she would get sick, too. Yolen worked as a summer intern at *Newsweek* magazine in New York City during the summer of 1959. However, she wasn't given a chance to write for the magazine.

Instead, she delivered mail, picked up coffee, sorted photos, and worked as a researcher and fact checker.

After her college graduation, Yolen broke up with her boyfriend, whom she had been planning to marry: "I needed to be free to explore my chances in the world of writing and publishing."[33] Jane was ready to move to New York City to begin her writing career.

After graduating from Smith College, Jane Yolen moved back to New York City in 1960. She rented an apartment in Greenwich Village with some friends. It was at their house-warming party that Yolen met her future husband, David Stemple. In this photo we see a picture taken in the 1960s of New York City's theater district.

3

Love, Career, and Marriage

YOLEN MOVED TO New York City in the summer of 1960. She rented an apartment with two other young women in Greenwich Village. During their housewarming party, Yolen met her future husband, David Stemple. David arrived at the party by climbing through a window. He introduced himself to Yolen by kissing her on the nape of her neck. According to Yolen, David told her he was a friend of one of the girls who lived in the apartment. "'I'm Jane Yolen,' was my icy reply. 'And I'm one of those girls. You're not my friend,'" Yolen recounted.[34] In spite of her reception, David wanted to get to know her better, and before long, they began dating. Yolen stated, "[It was] a slow-starting friendship and a long courtship."[35] Eventually, however, they fell in love.

They decided to live together in an apartment in Greenwich Village. Yolen didn't tell her parents she was living with her boyfriend. "My mother never knew—or at least never admitted to knowing—that my husband and I had lived together for a year and a half before we were married. Those were the days before such arrangements were the norm. . . . Mother would always call ahead when she and Daddy were coming to visit. We had plenty of time to hide the razor, the hairbrush, the men's clothes," Yolen recalled.[36] Perhaps Isabelle knew Yolen was sharing an apartment with David after all.

Meanwhile, Yolen was determined to pursue her dream of a writing career. "I considered myself a poet and a journalist/nonfiction writer," she stated.[37] She got a summer job in the research department at *This Week* magazine. When her summer job ended, she found a job at *Saturday Review* magazine. There she helped lay out the magazine for printing, chose cartoons, and decided how much space was available for poetry. Shortly before Christmas, Yolen was fired. She wasn't surprised because she had not been getting along with her boss. Nor did the news trouble her; she hadn't expected, or desired, to work at *Saturday Review* forever.

Yolen decided to become a self-employed writer in early 1961. She was hired to work on several projects. Her father, Will Yolen, was an international kite-flying champion. When he was asked to write a book titled *The Young Sportsman's Guide to Kite Flying*, he hired his daughter to research and ghostwrite the book for him. Yolen agreed to write the book, even though her name didn't appear on the cover. "I loved—and still love—the writing part best of all. It was no hardship, but the pay was very low!"[38] Yolen also wrote for several newspapers. She wrote short biographies of people for the *Celebrity Register*. She also wrote book reviews for *The New York Times Book Review.* Because she found it was hard to make enough money to pay her rent working as a freelance writer, Yolen also took a job as assistant editor at Gold Medal Books.

By this time, Yolen was thinking about writing her own books. She learned that a former teacher from Smith College had given her name to an editor named Judith Jones at Alfred A. Knopf publishing house. Jones wanted to see Yolen's work. Yolen lied and said that she already had a book ready for the editor to read. She thought children's books would be easy to write, so she set to work writing several children's books. She wrote an alphabet book of names, a book about kite flying, and a story about a whale that wants to be a minnow.

Yolen asked her artist friend Susan Purdy to draw some pictures to go with her stories. She also wrote out ideas for two longer books. One idea was for a book about real-life women pirates. This was an extension of a report she wrote for school in eighth grade. She also wanted to write a nonfiction book about kites that was longer and more in-depth than *The Young Sportsman's Guide to Kite Flying.* After Yolen and Purdy finished writing and illustrating the picture books, Yolen met with editor Jones. But Jones didn't want to buy any of her stories. "Of course I was crushed," Yolen wrote of the first time her work was rejected.[39] Purdy was upset, too. Together they sent the books around to several publishers, but no one wanted to publish the picture books.

Yolen's father offered to introduce her to his friend Eleanor Rawson. She was a vice-president at David McKay Publishing Company. Yolen agreed to meet Rawson. Rawson then introduced Yolen to children's book editor Rose Dobbs. Dobbs didn't like the picture books Yolen and Purdy had created; however, she did like Jane's idea for a nonfiction book about women pirates. She told Yolen she wanted to take some time to think about that idea. When Yolen finally heard back from Dobbs, the news was good. Although Dobbs didn't usually accept books from unknown authors, she took Yolen's proposal and agreed to publish the book when it was written.

Yolen's first book, *Pirates in Petticoats*, was accepted for publication on her 22nd birthday on February 11, 1961. "I was so excited that I ran down the three flights

Did you know...

In the early 1960s, Jane Yolen worked as an assistant editor at Alfred A. Knopf publishing house. As part of her job, Yolen met many other writers. She had the pleasure of working with Roald Dahl, author of the classic children's book *Charlie and the Chocolate Factory*. Yolen also worked with Ian Fleming, who is best known for his James Bond novels. Fleming wrote one children's book in the early 1960s, titled *Chitty Chitty Bang Bang*. The book is still popular with children today. Yolen wrote the book summaries that were used on the original back covers of both *Charlie and the Chocolate Factory* and *Chitty Chitty Bang Bang*.

of stairs and then ran three blocks to the Overseas Press Club, where my father was president and holding court at lunchtime. I said, 'Daddy! Daddy! I've sold my first book!'" Yolen recalled.[40] In celebration, Will bought everyone alcoholic drinks. Everyone except Yolen, that is. He bought her a Coke. "I was 22, and I was still his 'little girl'—which I remained . . . until the end of his days," Yolen remembered.[41]

Another important event in Yolen's life occurred in the early 1960s. Yolen married David Stemple on September 2, 1962. Their wedding was held in the garden at her parents' house in New Rochelle, New York. To welcome David to the family, Yolen's cousins showed up wearing fake beards to match David's real beard. The happy couple's wedding was fun and lighthearted with family and friends singing songs and celebrating. As a joke, Yolen sang a song called "I Wish I Were Single Again." Yolen's father was not sure Yolen should marry David. During the wedding, however, Will admitted she had chosen a good man. Yolen was happy that her father approved of her marriage. David's mother, Betty, had also worried about the marriage because the Stemples were Catholic and the Yolens were Jewish. "I received love and respect from . . . Betty—after she got over the shock of her Catholic son marrying a Jewish girl," Yolen recalled.[42] For their honeymoon, Yolen and David visited their sick grandmothers in Virginia and West Virginia respectively. They remain happily married today.

After her first two children's books were published, Yolen moved to Rutledge Press, a packaging house for children's books. She wanted to learn more about how children's books were created and published. Rutledge Press created children's books by hiring writers and illustrators. Then the publishing company sold the "package" to a larger publishing company, which would publish and sell the books to bookstores and libraries. While working at Rutledge, Yolen actually wrote a number of books that didn't have her name on them. She wrote rhymes for a book called *One, Two, Buckle My Shoe*. She also wrote games, puzzles, and activities for children's activity books.

Yolen had two children's books published with the David McKay Publishing Company in 1963. The first was *Pirates in Petticoats*, which tells the stories of famous women pirates such as Fanny Campbell, Anne Bonney, Mary Reade, and Madame Ching. She also published an illustrated book of poetry for children titled *See This Little Line*. Yolen disagreed with Dobbs about the color of the illustrations for *See This Little Line*. Dobbs chose the colors orange and purple, and so they were printed. Yolen stated, "We didn't see eye-to-eye on the visual look of the book, and she never bought anything from me again."[43] Nevertheless, Yolen credits Dobbs with helping her begin her career as a writer. "[I]t was her willingness to sit down with a young writer a year later and go over the completed manuscript, word by word by word, that started me on the path of publication," Yolen acknowledged.[44]

By the time her books were published, Yolen was creating books for Rutledge Press. Because she worked for Rutledge Press she was required to submit her new book ideas to the company before she submitted them anywhere else. "That was a major annoyance, though they never actually bought anything from me," Yolen commented on this condition of her employment contract.[45] Yolen still thought of herself as a poet, journalist, and nonfiction writer. She surprised herself when she began to write fiction. "It had never occurred to me that I could write anything fictional, because fiction writers were gods. They could

Jane Yolen and her husband, David Stemple, traveled through Europe during 1965–1966, including a trip to Greece. Above is a photograph of Thera, Greece, where Yolan visited. Yolen continued to write stories during her travels abroad.

take nothing and turn it into something, and I didn't have that ability, so I thought. It was a great surprise to me when I started writing fiction," she admitted in an interview.[46]

Yolen met an editor at Rutledge Press named Frances Keene. Keene eventually changed jobs, moving to the children's book department at Macmillan Press. After she left Rutledge Press, Keene asked to see one of the stories Yolen had submitted to Rutledge Press that had not been accepted. The book was titled *The Witch Who Wasn't*.

The Witch Who Wasn't is a story about a witch named Isabel who only knows good magic. This doesn't make her a very good witch at all, because witches are supposed to be bad. When Macmillan published *The Witch Who Wasn't* in 1964, the story received mixed reviews. *Book Week* called the illustrations "vulgarly ugly" and "dull" and the story "bland."[47] *The New York Times* liked the book better. The reviewer wrote that the illustrations were "comfortably comic" and called Isabel a "shrieking success" as a witch.[48]

On working with Keene, Yolen wrote, "It was the beginning of an editorial relationship that I *really* count as the start of my writing career. Keene . . . was a great teacher as well as a fine editor. She taught me to trust my storytelling ability."[49] Yolen preferred writing literary children's books over rhyme and activity books. She decided to leave her job at Rutledge Press and find a job at another publishing house where she might learn more about publishing children's books. Yolen got a job at Alfred A. Knopf publishing house as an assistant editor for juvenile books. She worked closely with editor Virginie Fowler. At Knopf, Yolen wrote book summaries to be published on the back covers of several popular children's books, including Roald Dahl's

Charlie and the Chocolate Factory and Ian Fleming's *Chitty Chitty Bang Bang.*

While Yolen worked at Knopf, she spent her spare time writing. She also formed a writer's workshop where young writers and editors could meet, share their work, and help each other with their writing. Members of the group included Jean Van Leeuwen, Alice Bach, Richard Curtis, James Cross Giblin, and Anne Huston. Although she had published a nonfiction book and several picture books, Yolen still thought of herself as a journalist. She wrote her first young adult novel, *Trust a City Kid*, with her friend Anne Huston. When asked about how she became a fiction writer, Yolen responded, "The first thing I wrote was the nonfiction book, and then I wrote a little picture book in rhyme. And then I wrote a fairy tale, and then I wrote another fairy tale, and then I wrote another fairy tale. And suddenly, I was a fairy tale writer. And that's sort of fiction. Then I wrote a novel with a friend, because I wasn't sure I could pull it off on my own. And that got published. I think I was just away then. It was so exciting that I could do it, that nothing could stop me after that."[50]

In 1965, Yolen met agent Marilyn Marlow and they agreed to work together. Marlow's job as an agent was to sell Yolen's books to publishers. She began trying to sell Yolen's work right away.

Yolen's husband David was very supportive of her writing career. David was busy, too. He worked with computers at IBM and worked on his own as a freelance photographer. He also made a point to read everything Yolen wrote, and still does. David has always been Yolen's first reader other than herself. Sometimes he suggests that she make certain changes in her stories. She only makes the changes if she agrees with his suggestions.

Yolen and David were very happy living in New York City for several years. Then they became bored with their busy lives and with New York City. They decided to quit their jobs and spend time traveling together. They spent a year saving money and planning their trip. David specifically wanted to travel to Greece, where he planned to take photographs. (The photographs would later be shown at West Virginia University.) Yolen and David also wanted to see the International Sheepdog Trials in Cardiff, Wales. "It sounded like fun," Yolen remarked.[51]

In August 1965, Yolen and David left the United States on a ship called the *Castel Felice* headed for Europe. "It was, without a doubt, the hippest ship afloat," Yolen declared in an essay about her life and work.[52] They joined their fellow passengers in various kinds of entertainment, including singing, plays, and poetry readings. Of course, Yolen brought her typewriter along and she tried to sit down and write every day during the trip. For most of their trip, Yolen and David traveled around Europe and the Middle East, going wherever they pleased. "We spent nine glorious months that way," Yolen reported in an autobiographical essay.[53] They visited tourist attractions and museums in Spain, France, Italy, and England. They also camped in a Paris park and swam in the Mediterranean Sea.

When Yolen and David reached Rome, they found that Yolen was pregnant. They were thrilled! They decided to continue their travels until the end of Yolen's pregnancy. They traveled from Italy to Israel, where they lived at a kibbutz (communal farm) for five weeks. Everyone who lives at a kibbutz is required to help with the work on the farm. Yolen picked oranges and shared songs with workers from Yemen. David picked bananas and worked on a chicken farm. Together they spent time snorkeling in the

Red Sea and living on the beach in Eilat. Finally, they moved on to travel in Greece for a month so David could take photographs for his upcoming show. The whole time they were traveling, Yolen was writing. She wrote many letters home to her mother about their trip. Her mother saved the letters into a notebook. Yolen and David still have the notebook. Yolen also wrote several stories that she hoped to publish when she returned to the United States.

Shown here is a typical street scene in New York City in the early 1960s. While living in New York City during the early 1960s, Jane Yolen worked for several publishing houses. She also had her first three books published, including the well-known title, Pirates in Petticoats.

4

Publishing and Parenting

YOLEN AND DAVID returned to the United States in May 1966. They were excited about becoming parents. For a short time, they lived with Yolen's parents in New York City while David hunted for a full-time job. Two days after their return, Yolen was called to a meeting with her literary agent Marilyn Marlow. When Yolen arrived at Marlow's office, Marlow had exciting news for her. "She had just sold three books for me—on the same day!" Yolen happily reported.[54]

Yolen's former editor, Frances Keene, bought her book called *It All Depends*. Yolen had written this rhyming book while she and David lived on the kibbutz in Israel. An editor named Ann Beneduce at World Publishing Company bought two other books, *The Minstrel and the Mountain* and *The Emperor and the Kite*. *The Minstrel and the Mountain* is an original folk tale about a minstrel (musician) who teaches two warring kingdoms about peace. *The Emperor and the Kite* tells how a young girl named Djeow Seow saves her father, the emperor, when he is kidnapped. She rescues him by sending him a kite attached to a rope. The rope was made of grass, vines, and her own hair. "The book is semi-autobiographical in that I had always wanted to please my father and never seemed to get it right," Yolen wrote of the inspiration for the story.[55] *The Minstrel and the Mountain* and *The Emperor and the Kite* were both published in 1967. *The Emperor and the Kite*, which was illustrated by Ed Young, was very well received. In fact, *The Emperor and the Kite* was Yolen's first book to win several major awards. It was named a Caldecott Medal Honor Book in 1968. The Caldecott Medal is awarded to the artist of the most distinguished American picture book for children. Yolen also won the 1968 Lewis Carroll Shelf Award for *The Emperor and the Kite*.

Yolen recalls her first meeting with editor Beneduce: "I met her that first week I was home, waddling into her office, eight months pregnant. Ann . . . became my friend from that first meeting . . . She *loved* fairy tales, and for the next 15 years or so, she was to be my major editor, publishing my first fairy tale collections and pushing me to try my wings in other genres as well."[56] Beneduce proved to be a tremendous influence on Yolen's career. She announced to the world that Yolen was "the American Hans Christian Andersen."[57] Yolen has always been slightly uncomfortable with this label. "I have always felt that claim quite a bit wide of the mark," Yolen admitted.[58] Nonetheless, Yolen and Beneduce worked well together. They worked together on 30 of Yolen's books.

Shortly after returning to the United States, David got a job at the University of Massachusetts Computer Center in Amherst. Yolen and David bought a house in Conway, Massachusetts. On July 1, 1966, Yolen gave birth to a daughter, Heidi Elisabet Stemple. The couple was absolutely delighted with Heidi. "Heidi was not my only production, however," Yolen declared.[59]

Yolen continued to write stories. "I found that having a new baby stimulated my imagination," she said.[60] Yolen had to learn how to juggle raising her infant daughter with her writing. Yolen's office was in the playroom. Heidi often sat happily in her playpen next to her mother's desk while Yolen worked. David, who was always supportive of his wife's writing career, helped Yolen whenever he could. He spent time with Heidi while Yolen worked. "He would cart Heidi off for long rides or walks in the woods, partly so that I could have time to write, partly so he could have more time with his daughter," Yolen stated.[61]

Baby Heidi inspired Yolen to write *Greyling*, a story about a childless couple that finds a seal on the beach. When they bring the seal home to take care of it, they discover it is really a selchie, a creature who is a seal in the water and human on land. The couple cares for the boy until he is a young man, when he rescues his father from the ocean during a storm. The young man turns back into a seal and he swims off on his own. "I began the book one night while nursing my new baby, Heidi, thinking about the time she'd be old enough to leave home," Yolen recalled.[62]

Yolen and David wanted to have more children. By 1967, Yolen was pregnant again. This time she had a miscarriage and lost the baby. She became pregnant again before the end of that year and she gave birth to a healthy baby boy, Adam Douglas Stemple, on April 30, 1968. In 1969, Yolen and David moved their family to Bolton, Massachusetts. They lived in Bolton for two years, during which time Yolen and David had a second son, Jason Frederic Stemple, on May 21, 1970.

Nine days after Jason's birth, tragedy struck. Yolen's mother Isabelle died from lung cancer. Isabelle had been diagnosed with incurable cancer several months earlier. Doctors told Will that his wife would only live for six months more. Will asked Yolen and her brother Steven not to tell their mother she was dying. Yolen recalled, "My father had begged my brother and me not to tell her, to support the fabrication that she had a nonlethal form of Hodgkin's disease. He said it was for her sake, but we both knew he couldn't bear to face her death head-on."[63]

Yolen saw her mother for the last time when she was seven months pregnant with Jason. Because she was having some difficulties with her pregnancy her doctor wouldn't let her travel. Therefore, Isabelle came to Bolton to visit her daughter. During their last visit, Yolen shared the manuscript of a picture book she wrote called *The Bird of Time* with her mother. She had started writing the book the

Did you know...

Jane Yolen worked at home while she raised her children. Her writing room was in the middle of the house, so she could write while she was taking care of her children Heidi, Adam, and Jason.

day she found out her mother was dying. In this original fairy tale, a boy can understand the speech of animals. He finds a bird that can speed time up, slow time down, or stop time completely. The bird helps the boy rescue a princess from an evil giant by adjusting the speed of time.

Isabelle understood that Yolen had written the story because she wanted to stop time. Yolen didn't want her mother to die. She is still sad that her mother never had the opportunity to meet her son Jason. "She died never having seen Jason, only a photograph of him I had sent special delivery from the hospital," Yolen wrote sadly.[64] After her mother died, Yolen missed her very much, especially when she wanted advice about raising her own children.

Raising her growing family didn't slow down Yolen's writing career. By 1970, Yolen had published 16 books, including *Gwinellen, the Princess Who Could Not Sleep*; *Isabel's Noel*; *World on a String: The Story of Kites*; *The Wizard of Washington Square*; *The Inway Investigators*; *Hobo Toad and the Motorcycle Gang*; and *The Seventh Mandarin*.

In 1971, Yolen and David moved to their family to a 14-room farmhouse in Hatfield, Massachusetts. "I wanted to call the place Fe-Fi-Fo Farm. But my wise and sensible husband David refused. . . . We called our house Phoenix Farm instead," Yolen wrote in her autobiographical picture book *A Letter from Phoenix Farm*.[65] Yolen's children suggested she write a book about Fe-Fi-Fo Farm. She later wrote a book called *The Giants' Farm*. The Giants in the book live on a farm called Fe-Fi-Fo Farm. While the family settled into Phoenix Farm, Yolen continued to write and publish books.

It was during this time that Yolen published several original fairy tales, including *The Girl Who Loved the Wind*, *The Girl Who Cried Flowers and Other Tales*, and

The Boy Who Had Wings. The Girl Who Loved the Wind is about a young woman whose father wants to protect her from unhappiness. The girl becomes a prisoner. The wind comes and visits her. He tells her about real life, about the good that can come of experiencing both happiness and sorrow. The young woman eventually escapes with the wind. One reviewer called *The Girl Who Loved the Wind* "a treasure."[66] Years later, Yolen realized the story was really about her leaving her family behind to marry David and begin her adult life. Yolen said, "A fifth grader at the Smith College Campus School pointed out to me that this was autobiographical since my father was overprotective and my husband and I met when he came in through the window of my apartment in Greenwich Village during a wild party."[67]

Yolen wrote the story for herself and for her family. But the story has touched many readers. Yolen once received a letter from a nurse. The nurse had read *The Girl Who Loved the Wind* to a dying girl. "[T]he story had eased the little girl through her final pain. The story did that—not me. But if I can continue to write with as much honesty and love as I can muster, I will truly have touched magic—and passed it on," Yolen wrote.[68]

Yolen's original fairy tales became popular. *The Girl Who Loved the Wind* won the 1973 Lewis Carroll Shelf Award. *The Girl Who Cried Flowers and Other Tales* was nominated for the National Book Award, a very important book prize, in 1975. While it didn't win the National Book Award, *The Girl Who Cried Flowers and Other Tales* won the Golden Kite Award from the Society of Children's Book Writers in 1974. "The publication of this book . . . established my reputation in the children's literature field," Yolen stated.[69]

Jane Yolen has been called "America's Hans Christian Andersen." While she was influenced by Andersen's tales, such as **The Arabian Nights,** *as pictured here, she does not feel altogether comfortable with the label.*

Yolen worked from her house while her children were growing up. Her writing room was located in the middle of the house. From there she found she could write while taking care of Heidi, Adam, and Jason. "I was already a published writer when my kids were born so I just kept on writing. They grew up thinking all mothers wrote," Yolen wrote in her online journal. "[W]hen I was writing, I was a great mom, making cakes, singing, telling stories. When I wasn't writing, I was grumpy."[70] Yolen and her family always had dinner together. People who were allowed to work in the family's barn making crafts during the day often joined the family for dinner. "[O]ur dinners were often huge affairs. The kids had other fascinating adults to hang with," Yolen reported.[71]

In the late 1970s, Yolen published more original fairy tales, including *The Seeing Stick, The Transfigured Hart, Moon Ribbon and Other Tales, The Simple Prince, The Sultan's Perfect Tree,* and *The Hundredth Dove and Other Tales. The Seeing Stick* is about a blind Chinese princess who learns to see with her fingers. Yolen calls this book "one of my own personal favorites."[72] *The Seeing Stick* won the Christopher Award in 1977. The Christopher Award is given to books that affirm the highest values of the human spirit. Yolen also wrote other kinds of stories, including the chapter book *Spider Jane* and an alphabet picture book titled *All in the Woodland Early. All in the Woodland Early,* which features drawings of birds, animals, and insects, was called "an outstanding alphabet book."[73] Music Yolen wrote to be printed at the end of the book allows readers to sing the story.

Despite her busy family life and her work, Yolen found time to get involved in other activities that were important to her. She joined the Religious Society of Friends (Quakers) in 1971. In 1972, Yolen published a book about Quaker founder George Fox titled *Friend: The Story of George Fox and the Quakers.* She hosted a monthly children's book writers and illustrators group at the Hatfield Public Library for 25 years. She also became active as a member of the Board of Directors of the new Society of Children's Book

Writers (SCBW) in 1974. "By being involved in all the SCBW activities, I began to feel that I was giving back— or rather paying forward—to all those folks who had helped me along the way," Yolen stated.[74] She organized conferences for the Society of Children's Book Writers for the next 10 years. Yolen remains a board member of the Society of Children's Book Writers to this day.

Yolen found time to go back to school in the mid-1970s. She got a Masters degree in Education at the University of Massachusetts. She also started a Ph.D. in Children's Literature. Yolen never completed the Ph.D., however, because she found that her writing career was becoming more and more demanding. Her original fairy tales were growing to be quite popular with readers, who wanted Yolen to write even more stories.

In 1988, Jane Yolen published The Devil's Arithmetic, *a story about a 12-year-old Jewish girl caught up in the Holocaust. Yolen wanted to help teach young people about this important historical event. The people pictured here behind fence and barbed wire are being held in one of the Nazi's many concentration camps.*

5

Dragons, Owls, and the Holocaust

"IT WAS IN the 1980s that I was discovered!" Yolen happily reported.[75] Suddenly, everyone was reading her stories. The short stories began appearing in science fiction magazines, anthologies, and textbooks. Storytelling became a popular way to share stories in the 1980s. Yolen began to get requests from people who wanted her permission to tell her stories at public gatherings. Her folk tales and fairy tales were especially popular. She continued to write original fairy tales, like *Brothers of the Wind* and *Dove Isabeau*. She also wrote several retellings of popular fairy tales, such as

Sleeping Ugly and *The Sleeping Beauty* (both retellings of *Sleeping Beauty*).

During the 1980s, Yolen also published humorous adventure stories, historical fiction, nonfiction, fantasy, science fiction, and mystery stories for young readers. In 1980, Yolen published *Commander Toad in Space*, the first book in her Commander Toad series. In this humorous story, Commander Toad and the frog crew of the Star Warts spaceship fight the evil monster, Deep Wader. The story contains lots of puns (words with more than one meaning) on the *Star Wars* movies. Yolen likes to inject humor into her stories and puns can be found in many of her books. One reviewer called the book "really funny reading."[76] Yolen wrote several more books for the Commander Toad series during the next decade: *Commander Toad and the Big Black Hole*; *Commander Toad and the Intergalactic Spy*; *Commander Toad and the Space Pirates*; *Commander Toad and the Dis-Asteroid*; *Commander Toad and the Planet of the Grapes*; and *Commander Toad and the Voyage Home*. The character of Commander Toad is based on Yolen's son Adam when he was young.

Yolen's historical books included the fictional story *The Gift of Sarah Barker*. In the story, two teens fall in love in a Shaker community in the 1850s. Shaker custom says it is a sin for men and women to have anything to do with each other. An accidental meeting brings Sarah and Abel together in a forbidden romance. Yolen has said of this book, "I always called this 'Romeo and Juliet in a Shaker community'."[77] Yolen was inspired to write the story when her daughter Heidi was a teenager. "I kept wondering how, in a Shaker community, you could keep the boys away from a girl like Heidi or keep Heidi away from the boys," Yolen recalled.[78] Yolen wrote a nonfiction book called *Simple*

Gifts: The Story of the Shakers to further describe life in a Shaker community.

Yolen also published the popular Pit Dragon series in the early 1980s. The series features the young dragon trainer Jakkin Stewart. In the first book, *Dragon's Blood*, 15-year-old Jakkin is a slave who takes care of dragons. His master is the best dragon breeder on the planet Austar IV. Jakkin steals a newly hatched dragon and hides it. He secretly trains the dragon, named Heart's Blood, to become a champion pit fighter. Jakkin earns enough money from Heart's Blood's fights to become a free man and a dragon master. Reviewers called the story an "original and engrossing fantasy"[79] and "splendid entertainment."[80]

In the second book in the series, *Heart's Blood*, Jakkin must rescue Akki, the girl he loves. Heart's Blood dies during the fight to save Akki from rebel forces. In the third book in the series, *A Sending of Dragons*, Jakkin, Akki, and Heart's Blood's baby dragons are hiding from the rebel forces. They discover a group of people hidden underground. These people like to kill dragons as part of a religious ritual. "I wrote the pit dragon books because I love dragons," Yolen has said.[81] The characters Jakkin and Akki are based on her children Adam and Heidi respectively. The Pit Dragon series is still very popular with readers and Yolen is currently working on a fourth Pit Dragon book.

Yolen likes to read mystery stories, just as her mother did. She decided to write several mystery stories for kids during the 1980s. First came *Shirlick Holmes and the Case of the Wandering Wardrobe* in 1981. In this book, Shirli and her friends solve the mystery of the missing antique wardrobe. Yolen thought about writing an entire series about Shirli and her friends, but it never happened. Instead, Yolen wrote a mystery series about Piggins the butler. In the first story, simply called *Piggins*, the butler is asked to solve the mystery of Mrs. Reynard's missing diamond necklace. *Picnic with Piggins* and *Piggins and the Royal Wedding* were published in 1988. Yolen would love to write more stories about Piggins. She hopes the Piggins series illustrator, Jane Dyer, will have time in the future to work with her on more stories.

In the late 1980s, Yolen published two books that established her as a distinguished children's author. In 1987, Yolen published a picture book titled *Owl Moon*. This is the story of a father and young daughter who search for an owl in the woods after dark. In an essay about the writing of the book, Jane wrote, "*Owl Moon* is a love letter to my family. . . . David is *Owl Moon's* Pa, and though each of the children suspects he or she is the . . . child of the story, I have to admit that I really had Heidi . . . in mind."[82] Five publishers rejected *Owl Moon* before Philomel Books finally accepted and published it.

Critics and readers alike loved Yolen's *Owl Moon*. A reviewer for *The New York Times* wrote, "[T]his book has a magic that is extremely rare in books for any age."[83] Even though *Owl Moon* sold many copies, Yolen didn't expect that her book would win any awards.

On January 11, 1988, *Owl Moon* received the Caldecott Medal. Yolen's friend Patricia MacLachlan, author of *Sarah Plain and Tall*, called her early in the day to tell her, off the record, that *Owl Moon* had won the Caldecott Medal. Yolen couldn't believe it, and she had trouble finding out if *Owl Moon* had truly won the award. Since the Caldecott Medal is given to the artist of the most distinguished children's picture book, *Owl Moon*'s illustrator John Schoenherr would be awarded the medal, not Yolen. According to the award rules, the winning book's artist must be notified before the author. However, Schoenherr was away on vacation and the award committee wasn't able to track him down until late in the day. In the meantime Yolen's agent Marilyn Marlow and editor Pat Gauch, who knew the truth, had to lie to Yolen all day. But she did tell Yolen to stay close by her phone. Finally, at five o'clock in the afternoon, Yolen knew she couldn't stand the suspense any longer. She called Gauch again. This time Gauch told her that *Owl Moon* had won the Caldecott Medal. "I may have screamed. I may have wept. I don't remember," Yolen wrote in the essay "On Silent Wings: The Making of *Owl Moon*."[84]

Yolen spent the evening celebrating with friends and her two sons, Adam and Jason. David and Heidi were on a trip to Ecuador, so they weren't home to celebrate, but Yolen told them the news when they called later in the evening. David was surprised and excited. Heidi was thrilled, but she wasn't surprised. She had told her father that she thought *Owl Moon* would win the Caldecott Medal.

Yolen called Schoenherr later that night to thank him for his wonderful illustrations. They celebrated the award together several months later. Yolen and David attended the Caldecott Medal ceremony in July 1988, when Schoenherr received his award. *Owl Moon* remains a beloved classic children's book today.

In 1988, Yolen published *The Devil's Arithmetic*, a story about a 12-year-old Jewish girl named Hannah Stern. When Hannah opens the door for the prophet Elijah during her family's Passover seder (Jewish home or community service including a ceremonial dinner held on the first or first and second evenings of Passover), she travels through time. She arrives in Poland in 1942, during World War II. The Nazis capture Hannah, who is now known as Chaya. Chaya is sent to a concentration camp, where she meets Rivka.

Rivka teaches Chaya to fight against the terrible conditions in the camps. She tells Chaya she must survive to tell the story of the Holocaust. Instead, Chaya takes Rivka's place when Rivka is chosen for the gas chamber. As Chaya enters the gas chamber, she becomes Hannah again and returns home to continue her family's seder.

Yolen found the novel hard to write. She had to do a lot of research about the Holocaust to learn about life in the death camps. "I actually DIDN'T want to write about the Holocaust, but some books just have to be written," Yolen stated in an online interview in 1998.[85] Yolen drew on her own experience as a teenager to create the character of Hannah. Like Hannah, Yolen didn't always enjoy learning about the Jewish religion. Yolen admitted, "Chaya is really me at that age: a bit whiney, a bit self-involved, a bit stubborn . . . a good storyteller, tired of learning stuff about being Jewish and yet fascinated, too."[86]

Critics praised *The Devil's Arithmetic*. Cynthia Samuels wrote, "Sooner or later all our children must know what happened in the days of the Holocaust. *The Devil's Arithmetic* offers an affecting way to begin."[87] *The Devil's Arithmetic* won the Jewish Book Council Award and the Association of Jewish Libraries Sydney Taylor Book Award in 1989.

Did you know...

Jane Yolen's father, Will Yolen, never read any of her books. He didn't think she was a real author, because in his opinion, real authors didn't write children's books. Due to her father's attitude towards her work, Yolen didn't have an easy relationship with her father. She desperately wanted to please him, but believes she often failed.

Yolen was amazed by the reactions to her book. "[I]t was the first book to take a child inside an actual death camp," she noted. "The reviews were stunning, the response overwhelming."[88] Yolen learned that *The Devil's Arithmetic* had been the most discussed book at the Newbery Medal meetings that year. The Newbery Medal is awarded to the author of the most distinguished contribution to American literature for children. "People were arguing and screaming. [The book] either makes people really, really moved or it makes them really, really angry . . . [T]here are many people . . . who feel that we should not tell our children about [the Holocaust], because it was such a horrible period," Yolen said in an interview in 1990.[89] *The Devil's Arithmetic* did not win the Newbery Book Award. Some people simply objected to the book's title. "*The Devil's Arithmetic* has been banned in some places because the word *Devil* is in the title," Yolen reported.[90] Yolen was especially touched by her daughter Heidi's reaction to the story. Heidi called her mother from college to tell her she thought it was "the most wonderful book in the world."[91]

In 1999, Dustin Hoffman and Mimi Rogers produced a movie based on *The Devil's Arithmetic* for the Showtime television network. Kirsten Dunst was chosen to portray Hannah and Brittany Murphy became young Rivka. Like the book, the movie version of *The Devil's Arithmetic* provides viewers with a disturbing look at life in the concentration camps of the Holocaust. Dunst said in an online interview that making the movie was hard work. "We shot it in Lithuania, and it was dark and depressing and freezing cold, even though we had warm stuff on underneath. . . . We could only imagine what these people really felt," she said. "We were shooting in the forest and only a few miles away they had burned all these Jews." The young actress returned to the United States a more mature woman. "It's the hardest I've worked and the most I've gotten out of a film," Dunst noted in 1999.[92]

Overall Yolen was pleased with the movie. She realized that it was necessary to make some changes to her story to turn it into a successful movie. "The film is strong on its own terms. But it is not the book, not entirely. And in places not even close. But that comes with the territory. In order to get it made, it had to be done with a fine young actress. Kirsten Dunst did a brilliant job—but she was already four years older than my hero, Hannah Chaya. So the changes began," Yolen said in an interview.[93]

Since she found it difficult to research and write about the Holocaust, Yolen decided she would not write about the Holocaust again. "When I was done, I swore to myself I would never write another book on the Holocaust because it was such an emotionally difficult task," Yolen said after writing *The Devil's Arithmetic*.[94] Therefore, Yolen was surprised when she found she had another Holocaust story that she needed to share with her readers.

She got the idea for her novel *Briar Rose* while watching the film *Shoah*, a 10-hour documentary chronicling personal remembrances about the Holocaust by dozens of survivors. In the film, the concentration camp Chelmno was described as a camp within a castle. To Yolen, the description suggested the fairy tale "Sleeping Beauty," but with much darker undertones. In *Briar Rose*, after her grandmother dies, Rebecca Berlin travels to Poland to find out why her grandmother believed she was a princess named Briar Rose. Rebecca learns about her grandmother's past in Poland during World War II. *Briar Rose* is written as a retelling of the Sleeping Beauty fairy tale. In the story, there is a concentration camp within a castle. *Briar Rose* was originally

Kirsten Dunst, picture here, played the role of Hannah Stern, the main character of Jane Yolen's book The Devil's Arithmetic, *when the book was made into a Showtime television movie in 1999.*

marketed to adult readers, but Tor Books published a paperback edition for teen readers in 2002. *Briar Rose* won the Mythopoeic Fantasy Award in 1993.

Some right-wing religious groups were offended by a homosexual character in *Briar Rose*. They banned the book.

One group in Kansas City actually burned the book on the steps of the Board of Education. Yolen responded to the censoring of her books with the following comments: "I think most of the time individuals or groups who want to censor or burn books do not read the books. Or do not read them all the way through. Rather they are on an action list of folks who will respond as they are told to do. Reading a book—and understanding it—takes time, attention, honesty, clarity, and an open mind. . . . We are . . . a nation that values freedom. And freedom to read what one wishes (or to not read) has to be an individual choice."[95] Despite the controversy surrounding *Briar Rose*, the book continues to sell well and is often used in both high school and college classes.

Yolen believes her books *The Devil's Arithmetic* and *Briar Rose* and the movie based on *The Devil's Arithmetic* help to teach young people about an important historical event. Young people need to know about the Holocaust. Yolen said in an interview, "[A]s we get closer to the time when people who were Holocaust victims are no longer with us, we're going to need this kind of evocation of memory. . . . [W]hat we need to do as adults is to point them toward the big signposts of history as well as we can and say 'These are the things you really need to know about.'"[96] Yolen hopes young people will read her books and watch the movie based on *The Devil's Arithmetic* and always remember the Holocaust.

Besides the awards given to *Owl Moon* and *The Devil's Arithmetic*, Yolen also received other important honors during the 1980s. In 1987, she won the World Fantasy Award for her collection of more than 150 folktales called *Favorite Folk Tales from Around the World*. Even though it was published in 1986, it is still used today by storytellers and by teachers of the art of storytelling. Yolen also won the

Kerlan Award for achievement in children's literature from the University of Minnesota in 1988.

In 1988, Harcourt Brace Jovanovich publishers hired Yolen to edit books by other writers. The books were published under the imprint title *Jane Yolen Books*. Yolen was mostly interested in publishing science fiction and fantasy stories. She published Bruce Coville's Magic Shop series, Patricia Wrede's *Enchanted Forest Chronicles*, Anne McCaffrey's *Black Horses for the King*, Kara Dalkey's *Little Sister*, Sherwood Smith's Wren series, and many others. While she worked for Harcourt, Yolen introduced the Magic Carpet Books paperback reprint line. She edited *Jane Yolen Books* for 10 years, until 1998. Harcourt continues to publish books in the Magic Carpet Books paperback reprint line.

Sadly, Yolen's father didn't live to see her become an important author and editor of books for children and young adults. In the early 1980s, Will suffered from the onset of Parkinson's disease. He came to live with Yolen's family at Phoenix Farm in 1982. Yolen and her family, with the help of hired nurses, took care of her father. Although Will lived with Yolen for the rest of his life, he never read any of his daughter's books. He never considered her to be a real writer. In his opinion, authors who wrote stories for children weren't real writers. After three years of round-the-clock care at home, Will Yolen died in 1985.

Yolen adored both her mother and her father. Her grief at the loss of both of her parents found its way into several of her books and short stories. In her young adult novel *The Stone Silenus*, Melissa must come to terms with her father's death after he commits suicide. *The Stone Silenus* was published in 1984, when Yolen's father was very sick. To this day, Yolen still loves and misses both of her parents very much.

One of Jane Yolen's historical fiction books is The Gift of Sarah Barker, *which takes place in a New England Shaker community in the 1850s. Pictured here is a barnyard at Sturbridge Village, a New England community that continues to value Shaker heritage.*

A Family of Writers

WITH THE SUCCESS of *Owl Moon* and *The Devil's Arithmetic*, Yolen's publishing career had reached new heights. However, she tried not to let her success go to her head. "I've won some awards, and I've made some money . . . it's no interest to me, because what I'm really interested in right now and passionate about are the books that I'm writing now," Yolen once said in an interview.[97] She continued to write picture books, fantasy stories, songbooks, poetry, and fairy tales for readers of all ages throughout the 1990s.

For the 500th anniversary of the discovery of the New World in 1992, Yolen was asked to write a picture book about the arrival of Christopher Columbus in the Americas. She chose to tell the story from the point of view of a young Taino Indian boy in *Encounter*. The young boy is scared of the new, strange people. He is afraid these men will hurt the Taino people, the pre-Hispanic inhabitants of the islands of Cuba, Haiti, the Dominican Republic, Puerto Rico, Jamaica, and the Bahamas. The story ends when the boy is an old man. He remembers his beloved people, whose lives and customs were destroyed by Christopher Columbus and the Spanish settlers.

Since the story is told from the point of view of the Taino, rather than that of the settlers, *Encounter* was considered controversial. The story of Columbus's arrival in the New World had never been told from the perspective of the Taino people. When she was first asked, Yolen was reluctant to write the story. She felt that someone from the Taino community should tell the story from their own per-spective. However, after doing some research, she realized that there weren't any Taino people left to tell the story. She decided to do it. Critics thought Yolen did a good job telling the story from the point of view of the Taino people. Reviewer Carolyn Phalen wrote, "[W]hile the portrayal of Columbus as evil may strike traditionalists as heresy, he did hunger for gold, abduct native people, and ultimately (although unintentionally), destroy the Taino. This book effectively presents their point of view."[98] Yolen said, "The book was the only one in that anniversary year to speak for the Taino people in a picture book edition."[99]

Yolen published several other picture books during the 1990s. *Raising Yoder's Barn* is a book about an Amish community that works together to build a new barn for the

Yoder family after their barn is lost in a fire. Young Matthew Yoder is happy he can help build the new barn by delivering orders to the workers.

In *The Ballad of the Pirate Queens*, Yolen writes about the story of the female pirates Anne Bonney and Mary Reade who sailed on their ship, *Vanity*. She had written about Bonney and Reade before in her first published book, *Pirates in Petticoats*. Bonney and Reade and the rest of the crew on *Vanity* were captured and put on trial. The male pirates were killed. In Yolen's version of the story, Bonney and Reade are set free because they are pregnant.

Yolen also wrote several poetry picture books for children. *Raining Cats and Dogs* is a book of poetry about cats and dogs. *Dinosaur Dances* moves towards the fantastic with poems about dinosaurs that dance the waltz, the rumba, and the tango. The dinosaurs also square dance and do the hula. Her book *A Sip of Aesop* introduces children to Aesop's fables and their morals through short poems and her book *What Rhymes with Moon?* features poems about the moon. When Yolen was growing up in New York City, she often had nightmares. "When we moved to the country, my bedroom windows looked out over trees and grass and flowers . . . I could see the moon. And seeing the moon, I stopped being afraid of the night," Yolen wrote in the introduction to *What Rhymes with Moon?*.[100]

Of course, Yolen also continued to write original fairy tales. *Good Griselle* tells the story of a Parisian woman whose soldier husband goes off to war. Griselle does good deeds, feeding the neighborhood birds and cats while she waits for her husband to return. Evil gargoyles test Griselle's goodness by leaving an ugly child on her doorstep. They expect her to turn the boy away. But although the boy is ugly, Griselle takes him in and loves and takes care of him. *The Girl in the Golden Bower*, another of Yolen's original fairy tales, tells the story of a child whose evil stepmother leaves her outside to die. Critics raved that Yolen "establishes the dreamy mood of an old-fashioned fairy tale."[101]

In 1993, Yolen compiled a collection of short stories and poems about dragons. It was published under the title *Here There Be Dragons*. The book includes the story "Cockfight," which Yolen has said was the beginning of the Pit Dragon trilogy. Several other *Here There Be* titles including poems and short stories about make-believe topics followed: *Here There Be Unicorns*, *Here There Be Witches*, *Here There Be Angels*, and *Here There Be Ghosts*.

Yolen has always loved the King Arthur stories. "If you ask me 'What was the greatest story ever told?' . . . I'd say King Arthur—with a little more emphasis on the girls."[102] By the middle of the 1990s, Yolen had written several books focusing on the mythical magician Merlin from the King Arthur legends. *Merlin's Booke*, a collection of short stories and poems, was published in 1986. In 1995, Yolen published a picture book about Merlin the magician called *Merlin and the Dragons*. When young King Arthur can't sleep, Merlin tells him a story that explains why he is destined to be king.

Yolen enjoyed writing about Merlin so much that she decided to write a fantasy trilogy for teens. The Young Merlin trilogy, including *Passager*, *Hobby*, and *Merlin*, was published in 1996 and 1997. *Passager* tells the story of Merlin when he is 7 years old. He lives by himself in the woods. He doesn't know how to talk. A falconer eventually takes him in, raising Merlin as his own. In *Hobby*, 12-year-old Merlin leaves after a fire kills the falconer and his family. Merlin becomes an apprentice with the magician

Ambrosius. He begins to discover his own magical powers. In the final book in the trilogy, Merlin is imprisoned when his magical powers are discovered. He escapes and meets a young child named Cub, who will later become King Arthur. A reviewer called the Young Merlin trilogy "a wonderful reworking of the legend of Merlin."[103] The trilogy won the Mythopoeic Fantasy Award for Children's Literature in 1998.

For many years, Yolen wanted to write a book about the idea that the world will end at a certain time on a certain date. She often noticed news stories about religious groups and cults predicting the end of the world before the next Millennium (the year 2000). At last Yolen decided it was time to write a story about a cult predicting the end of the world. She asked another well-known author of books for young adults, her good friend Bruce Coville, to cowrite

Did you know...

David Stemple, Jane Yolen's husband, published a nonfiction book for children about the wild turkey. It is titled *High Ridge Gobbler: A Story of the American Wild Turkey*. It was named an Outstanding Science Book for Children by the National Science Teachers Association when it was first published in 1979. Boyds Mills Press reprinted the book in 2001. It is available in bookstores and libraries.

Now that David is retired from his job at the University of Massachusetts, he spends a lot of time pursuing his favorite hobby, bird-watching.

the book. Together they created a story about teenagers Marina and Jed, whose parents are members of the cult called True Believers. Jed and Marina meet at the top of Mount Weepacut, where they are told that they will be able to survive the end of the world with their families and other True Believers. While Marina is a Believer, Jed is not. Despite their difference in opinion, they fall in love while waiting for the end of the world. Yolen wrote the parts of the story told from Marina's perspective, while Coville wrote from Jed's perspective. The book, titled *Armageddon Summer*, won rave reviews. One reviewer called it "a lovely piece of work."[104] *Armageddon Summer* was listed on many best book lists for young adult readers and it won the 2001 California Young Reader Medal.

Since Yolen and Coville don't live in the same town, it took them a long time to cowrite the book. They worked on it for about three years, meeting occasionally to write together. Most of the time, they faxed and emailed their parts of the book back and forth. Yolen says that the character of Marina is very much like her. "In many ways, Marina is me: full of passionately held beliefs that are often contradictory; loyal to family and friends but able to see others with a clear eye; [and] a big reader and quoter of poetry," Yolen wrote in an article about the writing of *Armageddon Summer*.[105] Similarly, the character of Jed is much like Coville when he was younger. "Bruce's character Jed is a wise guy who disguises his deeply felt feelings about family, and his intense intellectual preoccupation, with sass. He is Bruce at an earlier stage," Yolen informed readers.[106]

Although Yolen is well known as a fantasy writer, she began to write more from her personal and family experiences during the 1990s. She drew on her childhood experiences for two of her picture books, *All Those Secrets of the World* and *Miz Berlin Walks*. *All Those Secrets of the World* is the story of Yolen's life during the two years her father was away during World War II. The story begins with the departure of her father. Four-year-old Janie doesn't understand that her father, who left on a war ship, has gone far away. While they look at the ships sailing away from Chesapeake Bay, Janie's cousin Michael explains that the war ships look smaller as they sail further out to sea. Janie doesn't believe him. The ship her father sailed on was big. When Janie's father returns two years later, he says she looks bigger than he remembered.

> That's because you were so far away, Daddy.
> When you are far away,
> everything is smaller.
> But now you are here,
> so I am big.[107]

A reviewer wrote, "Yolen here relates a bittersweet memory from an important period in her childhood. . . . This timely nostalgic story is told with simple grace, and Janie's thoughts and experiences are believably childlike."[108]

Miz Berlin Walks tells the story of a young African-American girl named Mary Louise. One evening when she is bored, Mary Louise follows the elderly Miz Berlin on her evening walk. Mary Louise discovers Miz Berlin tells wonderful stories about growing up in Virginia. When Miz Berlin dies, Mary Louise knows she will always remember her. Yolen dedicated the book to her grandmother, Fanny Berlin, "who just plain loved to walk."[109]

Yolen also wrote books that are based on her family and family stories she heard growing up. Yolen's book called *And Twelve Chinese Acrobats* is a novel for middle-grade readers based on a Yolen family story about her Uncle Lou, Yolen's father's older brother. Lou is sent away to military school because he is a bad boy. He then disappears from school. His family worries. One day Lou returns home to Ukraine with 12 Chinese acrobats from the Moscow circus. Because Yolen always heard the story from her father, the story is told from Lou's younger brother's point of view. "The family was not amused. Or else they were. It depended upon which family member you asked," Yolen noted. "I am very fond of this book."[110]

Another picture book, called *Granddad Bill's Song*, is about a boy who is grieving the loss of his grandfather. When the boy asks each of his relatives what they did on the day Granddad Bill died, he is surprised by what he learns about his beloved Granddad Bill. One reviewer said, "This lovely book celebrates a life well-lived."[111] *Granddad Bill's Song* is loosely based on Will Yolen's life.

Yolen also wrote an autobiographical picture book in the early 1990s. In *A Letter from Phoenix Farm*, she wrote about her work, her family, her home, and her love of dragons. Yolen's son Jason Stemple provided the photographs for the book. This was the first book that mother and son worked on together.

Jason showed his mother his nature photographs. Yolen was inspired by the photos and asked him if they could write a book together. She wanted to write poems to go with his pictures. Jason suggested a water theme. *Water Music* was published in 1995. Yolen and Jason wrote several other books together during the second half of the1990s, including *Once Upon Ice*; *Snow, Snow*; and *House, House*. Yolen wrote the text of the poems while Jason took the photographs for the books. *Once Upon Ice* and *Snow, Snow* feature Yolen's poems and Jason's photos on a theme, just like *Water Music*. *House, House* features photographs of houses from the Connecticut River Valley, where Yolen lives. Historical pictures of the same houses, taken by the Howes brothers 100 years ago, are also included. Yolen compares the two sets of photographs of the houses, pointing out the changes that have taken place outside and around the homes over time. She and Jason also included pictures of their family's home, Phoenix Farm.

Yolen began to write books with her other children, Adam and Heidi, during the 1990s. Adam Stemple is a musician. He plays guitar and keyboard in a band called *Boiled in Lead*. While Yolen refers to Adam as "the *real* musician of the family," she too has always loved to write music.[112] They began writing music together when Adam was a teenager. Writing music helped him to cope with the ups and downs of growing up. They have written songs together for several books, including *Jane Yolen's Old MacDonald Song Book*, *Milk and Honey: A Year of Jewish Holidays*, *Jane Yolen's Mother Goose Song Book*, *Hark: A Christmas Sampler*, *Jane Yolen's Songs of Summer*, *The Lap Time Song and Play Book*, *The Lullaby Song Book*, and *Sing Noel*.

Yolen and her daughter Heidi began writing poetry collections and nonfiction books together in the mid-1990s. Heidi never planned to become a writer. "I never wanted to be a writer like my mother, Jane Yolen," Heidi has said. "But, after becoming a stay at home mom, I gave in and started writing, first with my mom and then alone as well."[113] In 1996, Yolen and Heidi wrote a picture book, *Meet the Monsters*, to pass the time while Heidi was pregnant. *Meet the Monsters* is a guide to identifying various kinds of monsters, including the Loch Ness Monster, golems, vampires, and werewolves. The book also includes instructions for how to get rid of these monsters. Since Heidi added the name Yolen to her own name when she was in college, she publishes her work under the name Heidi E.Y. Stemple.

In 1998, Yolen and Heidi published their first title in their Unsolved Mystery from History series. The books in the series examine real, unsolved mysteries. Jane and Heidi provide the many theories that exist about each mystery and readers are meant to draw their own conclusions using those clues. In the first book in the series, *The Mary Celeste*, Yolen and Heidi tell the story of a ship that was found drifting in the ocean. The crew was missing. No one knows what happened to the missing crewmembers. *The Mary Celeste* was well received. One reviewer wrote, "Fans of detective stories will be thrilled to try their hands at solving this true historic mystery."[114] Since the book was successful, Yolen and Heidi were asked to write more books about unsolved, real-life mysteries. The second book in the series, *The Wolf Girls*, is about two feral children who were found in India in the 1920s and brought to an orphanage. Yolen had been fascinated by the story of the wolf children for many years. She has written a novel, *Children of the Wolf*, a short story called "Wolf/Child," and two poems about the wolf children.

Next in the Unsolved Mystery from History series came *Roanoke: The Lost Colony*, about the British colonists who disappeared after settling in the New World in 1587. Critics have suggested that the Unsolved Mystery from History series helps make history interesting to children. Yolen and Heidi work very closely together on this series. Heidi reported, "My mother does the typing while I hold the research notes and tease her because she types with five fingers."[115]

There were some important additions to the Stemple family during the 1990s. Yolen and David celebrated the arrival of three granddaughters. Right after Yolen and Heidi finished writing *Meet the Monsters* in 1995, Heidi gave birth to her daughter Maddison Jane. Yolen made it to the hospital just before Maddison was born. She often says that Maddison is "named after her grandmother and an avenue."[116] In 1997, 14-year-old Glendon Alexandria Callan-Piatt moved in with Heidi, her husband Brandon Piatt, and Maddison. "I met Lexi by pure coincidence the day before my 31st birthday when she was 14 years old and in need of a new home," Heidi wrote in *Mirror, Mirror: Forty Folktales for Mothers and Daughters to Share.*[117] Heidi and Brandon were Glendon Alexandria's foster parents for several years. They adopted her in 2000, when she was 17 years old. In 1998, Adam and his wife Betsy had a daughter, Alison Isabelle. Yolen and David were absolutely thrilled with their grandchildren.

Jane Yolen fell in love with the Scottish countryside during her travels there. In 1994, she and David bought a house near St. Andrews, Scotland, and started spending summers there. This is a picture of St. Andrews castle. Yolen wrote the Young Merlin trilogy and the Stuart Quartet series of books in Scotland.

7

A Scottish Sojourn

YOLEN AND DAVID fell in love with Scotland when they traveled there for David's work. In fact, they loved Scotland so much that they eventually bought a house there. They began spending summers at their home in St. Andrews, Scotland, in 1994. Yolen calls their trips to Scotland their Scottish sojourn (temporary visit). Their house in Scotland is called Wayside. Yolen and David originally bought a half-interest in Wayside. But they came to love Wayside so much that they wanted to be the sole owners of the house. In 2005, they will hold complete ownership of Wayside. The rest of the Stemples often join Yolen and David for visits at Wayside during the summer months.

Yolen enjoys the slower pace of life she lives in Scotland. She likes being able to get away from the demands of her career in the United States for a time. She takes pleasure in going for walks in the Scottish countryside, having tea with friends, visiting castles and other historic sites, and spying on Scottish wildlife. Yolen uses her time in Scotland to recharge her batteries. Of course, she continues to write while staying in Scotland. Yolen enjoys writing so much she writes just about every day. "I still work there, in a lovely room that overlooks our garden," she wrote of working at Wayside.[118]

While at Wayside, Yolen wrote the Young Merlin trilogy and the picture book *All Those Secrets of the World*. She is often inspired by the Scottish landscape and the history that can be found in Scotland. Yolen has used Wayside as the setting for several other books, including *The Wild Hunt*, the books in the Stuart Quartet series, and the books in the Tartan Magic series. *The Wild Hunt* is an adventure story featuring two boys, an enchanted house, a talking cat, a conceited dog, and, of course, the Wild Hunt.

Yolen finds it much easier to write books for the Stuart Quartet series, which takes place in Scotland, while she is actually in Scotland. For one reason, the research materials she needs are more readily available. Another reason is that it's a lot easier for Yolen to meet with her Scottish coauthor, Robert J. Harris. Yolen wrote her share of the first book in the Stuart Quartet series, *Queen's Own Fool*, while at Wayside. *Queen's Own Fool* is the story of Mary Queen of Scots, told from the point of view of the female court jester (clown) Nicola. The book was well received. A reviewer for *Horn Book Magazine* called the book "a fascinating historical novel."[119]

Yolen and Harris were asked to write more such books. *Girl in a Cage*, the next book in the series, tells the story of young

Marjorie Bruce. Marjorie Bruce was the daughter of Robert the Bruce, who was the King of Scotland in the late thirteenth and early fourteenth centuries. Robert the Bruce wanted to free Scotland from the rule of England's King Edward I. King Edward held Marjorie captive to get the attention of her father. A reviewer for *Horn Book Magazine* said, "Marjorie is a believable heroine with whom readers will easily identify, proving once again that Yolen and Harris can really bring out the story in history."[120]

The third book in the Stuart Quartet series is called *Prince Across the Water*. In this book, Yolen and Harris tell the story of the Battle of Culloden, Bonnie Prince Charlie, and the hope of the Scottish people that the Stuarts regain control of Scotland. The story is told from the perspective of 13-year-old Duncan, who wants Bonnie Prince Charlie to replace King George as King of England. Duncan goes to war to fight for Bonnie Prince Charlie and he finds himself at the Battle of Culloden. "[T]his is a well-told story set in an intriguing era that will leave readers mulling over thoughts of war and peace," reviewer Anita L. Burkam wrote.[121] Yolen and Harris are currently working on the fourth book in the Stuart Quartet series.

Yolen uses the city of St. Andrews as the model for the make-believe town of Fairburn, Scotland, in her Tartan Magic series. This series is filled with magic, ghosts, dragons, unicorns, witches, and talking animals. In the first book of

Did you know...

When Jane Yolen isn't busy working, she enjoys taking walks and reading mystery stories. Sometimes she even goes bird-watching with her husband, David.

the series, *The Wizard's Map*, an American family visits Fairburn during the summer. Thirteen-year-old twins Jennifer and Peter Dyer have to rescue their little sister Molly from a wicked wizard. The wizard wants to trade Molly for an antique map they found. Reviewer Kay Weisman enthusiastically wrote, "The action never flags, making this a sure bet for fantasy and adventure fans."[122]

In *The Pictish Child*, the second book in the Tartan Magic series, Jennifer, Peter, and Molly visit a retirement home. In the graveyard behind the home, they meet a Pictish child who has traveled through time to try to change history. The Picts were ancient inhabitants of central and northern Scotland. Finally, in the third book in the series, *The Bagpiper's Ghost*, Jennifer and Peter get mixed up with the ghosts of two star-crossed lovers. The ghosts continue their feud with the man who kept them apart when they were alive.

When Yolen needs to do research for her books while in Scotland, she goes to the St. Andrews University Library. She also finds useful pieces of information in books she buys in old bookshops in St. Andrews. When Yolen is at her home in Hatfield, Massachusetts, she often goes to the Smith College Library to do her research. Yolen does a lot of research for her books. When asked about research in an interview, she responded, "I do lots and lots and lots. I am always researching. I read histories and biographies . . . folktales, bird books, and plant books, and flower books, and books about jewels. I am a researching fool."[123]

When Yolen is in Massachusetts, she mainly works in her attic writing room. She calls it the Aerie (eagle's nest). Yolen moved her writing room upstairs once her children became teenagers. She begins writing at 6:30 A.M. every morning. She drinks tea while she works. Yolen usually works the whole day, until 5 P.M. Besides writing, she edits books written by other authors, reads and answers her mail and email, and keeps in touch with her editors and her coauthors.

In July 2004, Yolen began writing an on-line journal that is part of her web site, *www.janeyolen.com*. She recently said in an interview, "In my entire life, I've never been able to keep a journal . . . I started writing something called *Telling the True: A Writer's Year*. And I've kept it faithfully. . . . But it's really more about what I'm writing than about my family. Mostly it's about the process of writing."[124] Yolen believes the Internet has changed her writing career in significant ways. She is more accessible to her fans. However, Yolen is cautious about using the Internet for research. "I do not yet trust the Internet for real research because in many instances I have no way of finding out if the research there is reasonable or accurate or true. But with my own web site, my fans or people who want to research about me will get the straight scoop," she reported in an interview in 2004.[125]

Being a writer involves lots of different kinds of work. Yolen enjoys her writing time most of all. "The absolute favorite part of being a writer for me is writing," she said in a video about her work.[126] Yolen often works on as many as 12 books at the same time. This helps her avoid writer's block. Whenever she gets stuck on something, she moves on to another book and goes back to the first one later. Or she goes for a walk.

Yolen often takes walks and has found that walking really helps her with her writing. "My favorite walk takes me by the Connecticut River. When I am walking I often get ideas for my books. Sometimes a problem that has been bothering me about a plot or character gets solved on these walks."[127] Sometimes Yolen goes walking just for fun, and often David or her friends join her. When she isn't working, she also enjoys reading, traveling, and visiting with family and friends. Yolen and David especially enjoy traveling and bird-watching together.

Above is a picture from the well-known story of Hansel and Gretel *(1812) by the Brothers Grimm. Jane Yolen enjoys retelling such stories. Her book* Sleeping Ugly *tells the story of an ugly princess who sleeps, adding new characters and a new spin to the original tale of* Sleeping Beauty. *Another of her books,* Briar Rose *also retells the story of* Sleeping Beauty; *however,* Briar Rose *is a more serious tale.* Briar Rose *uses the original fairy tale to tell a story about World War II Holocaust victims in Poland.*

8

Dinosaurs, Dollars, and Dances

YOLEN CONTINUES TO find her career to be both fulfilling and successful in the twenty-first century. In 2000, she found critical and commercial success with her picture book *How Do Dinosaurs Say Good Night?* Yolen's editor Bonnie Verberg asked her to write a book about dinosaurs for her son Robbie Verberg, who loved dinosaurs and hated going to bed. Yolen wrote of the book, "I was thinking of one dinosaur and his family. But Mark Teague, the illustrator chosen for the book, thought that doing one dinosaur over and over would be visually boring. . . . So he suggested doing different big lizards and different families."[128]

The result was the wildly successful *How Do Dinosaurs Say Good Night?* Each two-page spread features a different kind of dinosaur and his human parents. If you look closely, you will find the names of the dinosaurs on the pages. Sometimes the name is on the bed, sometimes on a wall hanging, or the blocks on the floor spell out the name of the dinosaur. Stephanie Zvirin wrote in *Booklist*, "The text is sweet and simple—just right for the wonderful pictures that really make this picture book special . . . A delight from start to finish." [129]

How Do Dinosaurs Say Good Night? spent eight months on *Publishers Weekly's* bestsellers list. It also spent five months on *The New York Times* best-selling children's books list. This was the first time that any of Yolen's books had spent such a long time on the bestsellers lists. *How Do Dinosaurs Say Good Night?* won the 2000 Christopher Medal. It was also listed on many best book lists for children in 2000 and 2001. *How Do Dinosaurs Say Good Night?* has been translated into many different languages, including Spanish, Korean, Dutch, Chinese, Brazilian, French, and Hebrew.

Yolen went on to publish several more Dinosaurs titles, including *How Do Dinosaurs Get Well Soon?*, *How Do Dinosaurs Clean Their Rooms?*, and *How Do Dinosaurs Count to Ten?* Yolen happily reported in a recent interview, "I hear from parents that their (not-yet-literate) youngsters want to hear the books over and over again!" [130] A fifth title in the series, *How Do Dinosaurs Eat Their Meals?*, is due out in 2005. Yolen is busy working on new title in the series called *How Do Dinosaurs Go To School?*

Yolen has recently published several other picture books. *Hoptoad* is the story of a toad that needs help crossing the road. *Harvest Home* began as a poem about harvest time. It turned into a picture book about a farm family at harvest time. "My husband, who as a boy used to take part in just such harvests on his grandparents' farm in West Virginia, says I got it just right except for the itch in the back of a sweaty neck caused by seeds. He is not an easy critic to please," Yolen noted.[131]

Yolen's granddaughter Maddison inspired her to write *Off We Go!* This book features many different animals making the trip to Grandma's house. "Maddison had the book memorized after the very first reading and proceeded to recite it for everyone," Yolen reported on her online journal.[132] The critics shared Maddison's enthusiasm. A reviewer wrote in *School Library Journal*, "It's bound to become a favorite with little people and the grown-ups who read to them, as well."[133] *Off We Go!* was named to several best-books lists, including the 2000 New York Public Library's One Hundred Titles for Reading and Sharing.

Yolen has recently published several fairy tales based on Russian folklore. *The Flying Witch* is an original fairy tale about a farmer's daughter who is captured by the witch Baba Yaga. The smart girl finds a way to force the witch to let her go. In *The Sea King*, a Russian king discovers he has promised his baby son to the Sea King. The prince grows up with the Sea King and has many adventures. Another picture book called *Firebird* is based on a Russian folk tale. In the story, Prince Ivan captures the beautiful Firebird in the forest. The Firebird promises to help him someday if Prince Ivan will let her go. The Firebird helps Prince Ivan battle the evil wizard Kostchei.

Yolen was very excited when she was asked to write about the Firebird folk tale. She remembers the story well from her childhood, when she dreamed of becoming a ballerina. "I first came upon the story of *Firebird* in the ballet, when Maria Tallchief as the Firebird and Francisco Moncion as

Prince Ivan performed in New York on November 27, 1949. The ballet was choreographed for the New York City Ballet Company by George Balanchine to music by Stravinsky," Yolen recalled.[134]

Yolen also has retold several other well-known folk tales in her books *Not One Damsel in Distress*. She wrote, "I chose stories that were fun, accessible, and that show young women as strong-hearted, quick-witted, and compassionate."[135] The book includes the story of Bradamante, the fierce medieval knight from *The Song of Roland*. Yolen also wrote about Li Chi, a Chinese girl who slays a dreaded serpent. In another story based on an English folk tale, Burd Janet rescues her true love Tam Lin from the queen of the faeries. Three years later, Yolen wrote *Mightier Than the Sword*, a companion book to *Not One Damsel in Distress*. For the book, she said, "I wanted stories in which the boys never pick up a sword and chop off the villain's head."[136] She discovered it was difficult to find stories where the boys use their brains to defeat their enemies. Yolen worked hard to find stories to include in this book. Both *Not One Damsel in Distress* and *Mightier Than the Sword* were very well received, winning high praise and awards.

Yolen also began writing a new series with her Stuart Quartet series coauthor Robert J. Harris. The Young Heroes series features popular heroes from ancient Greece, such as Odysseus, Hippolyta, Atalanta, and Jason, in their early teens. The series began with the book *Odysseus in the Serpent Maze*. Thirteen-year-old Odysseus, his best friend Mentor, his future wife Penelope, and her cousin Helen are all kidnapped by pirates. This is the beginning of an exciting adventure for the group as Odysseus helps them find their way home. In *Hippolyta and the Curse of the Amazons*, the young Amazon Hippolyta learns to accept the love and help of a boy in order to save the Amazons. *Atalanta and the Arcadian Beast* recounts the story of Atalanta, who lives in the woods with the animals. When a nasty beast terrorizes the Arcadian lands, Atalanta joins an expedition led by the hunter Orion to capture the beast. In *Jason and the Gorgon's Blood*, several young warriors, including Jason, are asked to save the kingdom of Iolcus from a horrible fate. One reviewer praised the series, writing that "the authors may well draw boys and girls in equal numbers—and send them clamoring for more Greek myths."[137] Despite the popularity of the Young Heroes series, *Jason and the Gorgon's Blood* will be the final book in the series.

In 2003, Yolen finally published the King Arthur novel she had been working on for more than 16 years. *Sword of the Rightful King* is her version of the familiar Arthurian Sword in the Stone legend. In Yolen's story Morgause, Queen of Orkney, wants one of her sons to win the crown from King Arthur. Merlin the magician comes up with the Sword in the Stone myth, and with a little help, young King Arthur uses the new myth to hold on to his crown. *Sword of the Rightful King* won rave reviews. It has been named to many best-books lists for young adults.

Despite the popularity of many of Yolen's books, not all her books get great reviews. How does she deal with bad reviews? "I handle negative notices badly. I curse. I take a hot shower. And then I get back to work," Yolen reported in an interview.[138] Sometimes publishers have not liked her books. If a publisher decides not to publish something an author has written, the publisher sends the author a rejection letter. Even after 40 years as a published writer, Yolen still receives rejection letters from publishers. But she knows rejection is just part of the publishing business. When Yolen opens a rejection letter, she doesn't worry about it too much.

In 2000, Jane Yolen published the wildly successful book How Do Dinosaurs Say Good Night? *The book, which makes dinosaurs more humorous than scary, as pictured here, won the 2000 Christopher Award and has been translated into many different languages.*

She just carries on with the new books she is writing. Marilyn Marlow was Yolen's literary agent for 38 years. Her long-time assistant, Elizabeth Harding, is now Yolen's agent and Harding continues to sell many of Yolen's books to various publishers. When one publisher rejects a book, Harding will try to sell the book to another. Sometimes it works out. Still, Yolen has many unpublished books on her desk.

Yolen continues to write books with her now-adult children. In 2002, Heidi and her daughters Glendon and Maddison moved to Phoenix Farm to live with Yolen and David. According to Yolen, "Heidi was worried about her parents aging. And she wanted better schools for her kids." [139] Yolen now shares her office in the attic, the Aerie, with Heidi. When working together, Heidi notes, "All I have to do is yell into the next room since my mother is being nice enough to share her office with me." [140] Sometimes Yolen and Heidi still share their work with one another over email, even though they work in the same office. Besides the books she has written with Yolen, Heidi has written poetry, short stories, and books on her own.

Heidi likes working with her mother nearby. On working with Yolen, Heidi has said, "My mother inspires me every day because of her love of her art and because she lights a fire under me if I'm not working hard or fast enough." [141] Everyone close to Yolen knows how hard she works on her writing. Yolen has inspired all her children, including Heidi, to write. "I can't imagine any better footprints to walk in. . . .

Did you know...

For the last 18 years, Jane Yolen has sponsored the Jane Yolen Writing Contest at the Hatfield Elementary School in her hometown of Hatfield, Massachusetts. Yolen reads all of the contest entries. She gives awards for poetry, prose, and nonfiction. Yolen looks for writing that speaks from the heart. Hatfield Elementary School recently named their reading room the Jane Yolen Reading Room.

My mother is wise and witty. Talented, too. And, in my view, all-knowing," Heidi once wrote about Yolen.[142] When asked what it is like working with her children, Yolen responded, "I am in awe of their talents; they are in awe of my work ethic."[143]

In 2004, Yolen and Heidi published another title in their Unsolved Mystery from History series. *The Salem Witch Trials* looks at the hysteria surrounding the witch hunts in Salem, Massachusetts, in 1692. Yolen and Heidi are still working on new titles in their Unsolved Mystery from History series, including a book on Amelia Earhart.

Yolen and Heidi have also written poetry and fairy tales together focusing on a mother-daughter theme. They published a book of poetry called *Dear Mother, Dear Daughter: Poems for Young People* in 2001. The poems are really notes from Heidi combined with Yolen's responses. Topics covered in the poems include wanting to pierce ears, needing a raise in allowance, feeling fat, homework, curfew, the death of a grandmother, and seeing a gun in a school locker.

In 2000, Yolen and Heidi published a collection of fairy tales and folktales. *Mirror, Mirror: Forty Folktales for Mothers and Daughters to Share* features stories about strong mothers, grandmothers, obsessive mothers, wicked stepmothers, and doting mothers. A conversation about the story between Yolen and Heidi follows each tale. Both Yolen and Heidi admit that they are a bit embarrassed by how much of themselves they reveal in these conversations. But writing the book gave them a chance to get to know each other better.

More recently, Yolen and Heidi published *The Barefoot Book of Ballet Stories*. This book includes seven ballets, such as *Swan Lake*, *The Nutcracker*, and *The Sleeping Beauty*. Each ballet is introduced with some information about the history of the dance. The Amherst Ballet recently performed a newly choreographed version of the ballets *Shim Chung* and *Swan Lake*. The ballets are based on the stories in *The Barefoot Book of Ballet Stories*. Yolen and Heidi narrated the stories and Maddison danced in *Shim Chung*.

Yolen continues to work with her sons Adam and Jason. Jason took photographs to go along with Yolen's poetry in several collections, including *Color Me a Rhyme*, *Horizon*, *Wild Wings*, *Least Things*, and *Fine Feathered Friends*. They won the 2002 National Outdoor Book Award for *Wild Wings* and are working on new books of Yolen's poetry and Jason's photographs. Yolen and Adam are currently working on the music for several new songbooks. They also have written a novel together called *Pay the Piper*.

Yolen won several important awards for her work in 2003. She won the National Storytelling Network Oracle Award for outstanding contributions to the literary body of storytelling. She was also given an honorary Doctorate degree from her alma mater, Smith College.

The Stemple family has continued to grow. Adam and his wife Betsy had a son, David Francis, in 2002. Jason and his wife Joanne had twin girls, Caroline Lee and Amelia Hyatt, in 2003. While the new additions to the family were welcome, the Stemples also dealt with an unwelcome event in 2002. Jane's husband David was diagnosed with an inoperable brain tumor. He had successful radiation treatment that shrank the tumor, and he remains healthy today. Yolen dealt with this difficult time in her life by writing a series of poems that were published in a book for adult readers titled *The Radiation Sonnets*. Once David was feeling better, the Stemples got back to their regular schedule, living in Scotland during the summer and residing in Massachusetts during the rest of the year.

The first book in The Pit Dragon trilogy, Dragon's Blood, *was published in 1982. In this first book we meet Jakkin, a young boy who secretly trains a dragon in hopes of winning his freedom.* Heart's Blood *followed in 1984, and the final book in the trilogy,* A Sending of Dragons, *was published in 1987. Readers of the trilogy have asked Jane Yolen time and again for another Pit Dragon book, so Yolen is currently working on a fourth book.*

9

An Extraordinary Career

EVEN AFTER MORE than 40 years as a professional writer, Yolen continues to love to write. She still follows a regular schedule, working every day writing books and poems, editing other people's books, and composing speeches for speaking engagements. While she continues to make regular appearances at conferences, her busy writing, traveling, and family schedule do not leave her much time for school visits anymore. However, her daughter, Heidi E.Y. Stemple, who is following in her mother's footsteps as a writer, visits schools and talks to students about writing on her own and writing with her mother.

Yolen also participates in a weekly women's writing group that she started in the early 1970s. Group members, who are all published authors, include Patricia MacLachlan, Corinne Demas Bliss, Anna Kirwan, Barbara Diamond Goldin, and Lesléa Newman. The writers meet to share their work and help each other with their writing. Since publishing can be a tough business, they also offer each other moral support.

Yolen has many more ideas for books she wants to write and plans to continue writing for years to come. She stated in an interview, "A writer doesn't run out of ideas—a writer runs out of time." [144] Yolen is currently writing several new books. She was recently asked to write a new book about women pirates. Yolen is also working on a new book about Jakkin and Akki, since so many of her fans have asked for another Pit Dragon book. (Of course, this will make the Pit Dragon series a tetralogy, instead of a trilogy.) The book is tentatively titled *Dragon's Heart*.

Did you know...

Jane Yolen has been called the "American Hans Christian Andersen." Hans Christian Andersen wrote many popular fairy tales, including *The Princess and the Pea*, *The Ugly Duckling*, and *The Emperor's New Clothes*. Since Yolen was born into a Jewish family, she jokes that she is the "Hans Jewish Andersen."

Jane Yolen Official Web Site. *www.janeyolen.com.*

Jane Yolen Official Web Site, Jane Yolen's Nonfiction: *The Perfect Wizard. www.janeyolen.com/blurbs/perfectw2.html.*

Fans of Yolen's work will be able to find several new books by the author in 2005. She was asked to write a biography of children's writer Hans Christian Andersen. Her book *The Perfect Wizard: Hans Christian Andersen* was chosen to be one of the official books of the celebration of the writer's 200th birthday in 2005. Yolen also published another family story, *Grandma's Hurrying Child*, which tells the story of her granddaughter Maddison's birth 10 years ago. Yolen rushed by plane and taxi to get to the hospital in time for Maddison's birth. Other new picture books by Yolen that are due out in 2005 include *Soft House* and *How Do Dinosaurs Eat Their Meals?* A collection of stories about cats, Yolen's favorite animal, will be available in her new book *Meow: Cat Tales from Around the World*.

Yolen also has several new books she wrote with her children scheduled to publish in 2005. She and Adam wrote a novel called *Pay the Piper*. They also have two new songbooks, *Trot, Trot to Boston* and *Apple for the Teacher*. She and Jason have a new poetry book due out, featuring Jason's photographs, called *Count Me a Rhyme*.

Yolen still finds inspiration for her stories all around her. She has even based characters on her friends and members of her family. But she realizes that in order to write as she does she must concentrate on what she can give to her stories. Yolen said in a video about her work, "I think the person who figures the most in my stories is me. Me as I'd like to be, me as I'm afraid I am. Me."[145] Yolen writes her books for herself first, since she is the first person to read them. Once she is happy with her work, she thinks about the other people who will read her stories. First she makes sure she writes a good story, and then she thinks about her readers.

Yolen enjoys the many roles she plays in her life, but she enjoys spending time with her family, especially her grandchildren, and her writing time most of all. She has declared, "Even if I weren't paid for the writing that I do, I'd still be writing. Writing isn't just my business, it isn't just my vocation, it's my life."[146]

Jane Yolen has had an absolutely extraordinary writing career. She has published more than 250 books and won many awards and honors. Yolen doesn't spend a lot of time thinking about her published books or her status as a famous author, but rather about the stories she wants to write in the future. She reflected on her career an autobiographical essay: "I consider myself a poet and a storyteller. Being 'America's Hans Christian Andersen' means trying to walk in much-too-large seven-league boots. I just want to go on writing and discovering my stories for the rest of my life because I know that in my tales I make public what is private, transforming my own joy and sadness into tales for the people."[147]

1 Jane Yolen Official Web Site, Jane Yolen's Picture Books: *Firebird*. *www.janeyolen.com/blurbs/firebird2.html*.

2 Jane Yolen Official Web Site.*www.janeyolen.com*.

3 Quoted in Alan Hedblad, ed. "Jane Yolen: Autobiography Feature." *Something About the Author* vol. 111 (Detroit, MI: Gale Group, 2000), 203.

4 Jane Yolen, Billie Judy, and Jonathan Stratman, *The Children's Writer at Work Featuring Jane Yolen*. VHS (Bainbridge Island, WA: Reel Life Productions, 1997).

5 Quoted in Alan Hedblad, ed. "Jane Yolen: Autobiography Feature." *Something About the Author* vol. 111, 205.

6 Ibid.

7 Ibid.

8 Jane Yolen and Heidi E.Y. Stemple, *Mirror, Mirror: Forty Folktales for Mothers and Daughters to Share* (New York: Viking, 2000), xvii.

9 Quoted in Alan Hedblad, ed. "Jane Yolen: Autobiography Feature." *Something About the Author* vol. 111, 206.

10 Ibid.

11 Jane Yolen, *All Those Secrets of the World* (Boston: Little, Brown and Company, 1991), 22.

12 Jane Yolen Official Web Site, Jane Yolen Biography: "A Short Biography". *www.janeyolen.com/janebio.html*.

13 Reading Rockets: Reading Rockets Interview with Jane Yolen. *www.readingrockets.org/transcript.php?ID=76*.

14 Ibid.

15 Quoted in Alan Hedblad, ed. "Jane Yolen: Autobiography Feature." *Something About the Author* vol. 111, 206.

16 Ibid.

17 Scholastic.com, AuthorsandBooks: Author Booklist, "Jane Yolen's Interview+transcript". *www2.scholastic.com/teachers/authorsandbooks/authorstudies/authorhome.jhtml?authorID=215&collateralID=6664&displayName=Interview%2Btranscript*.

18 Quoted in Alan Hedblad, ed. "Jane Yolen: Autobiography Feature." *Something About the Author* vol. 111, 206.

19 Jane Yolen Official Web Site, Jane Yolen Biography: "A Short Biography."

20 Quoted in Alan Hedblad, ed. "Jane Yolen: Autobiography Feature." *Something About the Author* vol. 111, 207–208.

21 Ibid., 208.

22 Ibid.

23 Ibid.

24 Jane Yolen and Heidi E.Y. Stemple. *Mirror, Mirror: Forty Folktales for Mothers and Daughters to Share*, 56.

25 Ibid., 52.

NOTES

26 Quoted in Alan Hedblad, ed. "Jane Yolen: Autobiography Feature." *Something About the Author* vol. 111, 208.

27 Ibid.

28 Jane Yolen and Heidi E.Y. Stemple. *Mirror, Mirror: Forty Folktales for Mothers and Daughters to Share*, xvii.

29 Jane Yolen Official Web Site, Jane Yolen Biography: "A Short Biography."

30 Quoted in Alan Hedblad, ed. "Jane Yolen: Autobiography Feature." *Something About the Author* vol. 111, 209.

31 Jane Yolen Official Web Site, Jane Yolen Biography: "A Short Biography."

32 Quoted in Alan Hedblad, ed. "Jane Yolen: Autobiography Feature." *Something About the Author* vol. 111, 209.

33 Jane Yolen and Heidi E.Y. Stemple. *Mirror, Mirror: Forty Folktales for Mothers and Daughters to Share*, 168.

34 Quoted in Alan Hedblad, ed. "Jane Yolen: Autobiography Feature." *Something About the Author* vol. 111, 210.

35 Ibid.

36 Jane Yolen and Heidi E.Y. Stemple. *Mirror, Mirror: Forty Folktales for Mothers and Daughters to Share*, xvi.

37 Jane Yolen Official Web Site, Jane Yolen Biography: "A Short Biography."

38 Quoted in Alan Hedblad, ed. "Jane Yolen: Autobiography Feature." *Something About the Author* vol. 111, 210.

39 Ibid., 211.

40 Reading Rockets: Reading Rockets Interview with Jane Yolen.

41 Ibid.

42 Jane Yolen and Heidi E.Y. Stemple. *Mirror, Mirror: Forty Folktales for Mothers and Daughters to Share*, 195.

43 Quoted in Alan Hedblad, ed. "Jane Yolen: Autobiography Feature." *Something About the Author* vol. 111, 212.

44 Ibid.

45 Ibid., 213.

46 Reading Rockets: Reading Rockets Interview with Jane Yolen.

47 M.S. Libby, "Yolen, Jane. *The Witch Who Wasn't.*" *Book Week* (October 25, 1964), 16.

48 Margaret F. O'Connell, "Books for Young Readers: *The Witch Who Wasn't.*" *The New York Times* (October 25, 1964), BR36.

49 Quoted in Alan Hedblad, ed. "Jane Yolen: Autobiography Feature." *Something About the Author* vol. 111, 213.

50 Reading Rockets: Reading Rockets Interview with Jane Yolen.

51 Quoted in Alan Hedblad, ed. "Jane Yolen: Autobiography Feature." *Something About the Author* vol. 111, 214.

52 Ibid.

53 Ibid.

54 Ibid.

55 Jane Yolen Official Web Site, Jane Yolen's Picture Books: *The Emperor and the Kite*. *www.janeyolen.com/blurbs/ emperoratk2.html*.

56 Quoted in Alan Hedblad, ed. "Jane Yolen: Autobiography Feature." *Something About the Author* vol. 111, 215.

57 Ibid.

58 Ibid.

59 Ibid.

60 Ibid., 216.

61 Ibid.

62 Jane Yolen Official Web Site, Jane Yolen's Picture Books: *Greyling*. *www.janeyolen.com/blurbs/ greyling2.html*.

63 Jane Yolen and Heidi E.Y. Stemple. *Mirror, Mirror: Forty Folktales for Mothers and Daughters to Share*, xvi.

64 Quoted in Alan Hedblad, ed. "Jane Yolen: Autobiography Feature." *Something About the Author* vol. 111, 217.

65 Jane Yolen, *A Letter from Phoenix Farm* (Katonah, NY: Richard C. Owen Publishers, Inc., 1992), 5.

66 Marilyn R. Singer, review of *The Girl Who Loved the Wind*. *School Library Journal* (March 1973), 102.

67 Jane Yolen Official Web Site, Jane Yolen's Picture Books: *The Girl Who Loved the Wind*. *www.janeyolen.com/blurbs/girl-wltw2.html*.

68 Quoted in Alan Hedblad, ed. "Jane Hyatt Yolen," *Something About the Author* vol. 112 (Detroit, MI: Gale Group, 2000), 217.

69 Jane Yolen Official Web Site, Jane Yolen's Picture Books: *The Girl Who Cried Flowers and Other Tales. www.janeyolen.com/blurbs/ girlwcf2.html*.

70 Jane Yolen Official Web Site, Journal Dec 2004: *Telling the True: A Writer's Journal*. December 6, 2004. *www.janeyolen.com/journal. html*.

71 Ibid.

72 Jane Yolen Official Web Site, Jane Yolen's Picture Books: *The Seeing Stick. www.janeyolen.com/ blurbs/seeings2.html*.

73 Review of *All in the Woodland Early*. *Publishers Weekly* (January 11, 1980), 88.

74 Quoted in Alan Hedblad, ed. "Jane Yolen: Autobiography Feature." *Something About the Author* vol. 111, 218.

75 Ibid., 219.

76 Judith Goldberger, review of *Commander Toad in Space*. *Booklist* (November 15, 1980), 464.

77 Jane Yolen Official Web Site, Jane Yolen's Picture Books: *The Gift of Sarah Barker. www.janeyolen .com/blurbs/giftosb2.html*.

78 Quoted in Tracey Watson, ed. "Jane Hyatt Yolen," *Contemporary Authors: New Revision Series* vol. 126, (Detroit, MI: Gale Research, Inc., 2004), 446.

79 Ann A. Flowers, review of *Dragon's Blood*, *Horn Book* (August 1982), 418–419.

80 Pauline Thomas, review of *Dragon's Blood*, *School Librarian* (December 1983), 384.

81 Jane Yolen Official Web Site, Jane Yolen's Picture Books: *Dragon's Blood*. *www.janeyolen.com/blurbs/dragonsb2.html*.

82 Jane Yolen, "On Silent Wings: The Making of *Owl Moon*," *The New Advocate* 2, no. 4 (Fall 1989), 199.

83 Paul Johnson, "Review of *Owl Moon*," *The New York Times* (January 3, 1988), BR23.

84 Jane Yolen, "On Silent Wings: The Making of *Owl Moon*," 210.

85 Jane Yolen. *www.readin.org/authors/archives/1998/Jane_Yol.htm*.

86 DownHomeBooks.com, Author Interviews: January 2004 Jane Yolen. *www.downhomebooks.com/yolen.htm*.

87 Cynthia Samuels, "Hannah Learns to Remember," *The New York Times* (November 13, 1988), BR62.

88 Quoted in Alan Hedblad, ed. "Jane Yolen: Autobiography Feature." *Something About the Author* vol. 111, 219.

89 Quoted in Hal May and James G. Lesniak, ed., "Jane Hyatt Yolen," *Contemporary Authors, New Revision Series* vol. 29 (Detroit, MI: Gale Research, Inc., 1990), 468.

90 Jane Yolen and Bruce Coville, "Two Brains, One Book: Or How We Found Our Way to the End of the World," *Book Links* 8, no. 2, (November 1998), 58.

91 Quoted in Hal May and James G. Lesniak, ed., "Jane Hyatt Yolen," *Contemporary Authors, New Revision Series* vol. 29, 468.

92 Gerri Miller, "Kirsten Dunst: On How Playing a Jewish Girl in *The Devil's Arithmetic* Changed Her Life." *www.jvibe.com/popculture/dunst.shtml*.

93 Susanna Daniel, *Jane Yolen. The Library of Author Biographies* (New York: Rosen Publishing Group, Inc., 2004), 72.

94 Rosetta Stone. "A Book Review and Discussion with Jane Yolen, Author." *www.underdown.org/yolen.htm*.

95 Ibid.

96 Peter Applebome, "The Devil's Arithmetic: Memories Count," *The New York Times* (March 28, 1999), 13.3.

97 Reading Rockets: Reading Rockets Interview with Jane Yolen. *www.readingrockets.org/transcript.php?ID=76*.

98 Carolyn Phalen, "Fiction—Encounter by Jane Yolen and Illustrated by David Shannon," *Booklist* 88, no. 13 (March 1, 1992), 1281.

99 Jane Yolen Official Web Site, Jane Yolen's Picture Books: *Encounter. www.janeyolen.com/ blurbs/encounter2.html.*

100 Jane Yolen, *What Rhymes with Moon?* (New York: Philomel, 1993), 7.

101 Elizabeth Devereaux and Diane Roback, "Children's Books—The Girl in the Golden Bower by Jane Yolen and illustrated by Jane Dyer," *Publishers Weekly* 241, no. 33 (August 15, 1994), 95.

102 John Koch, "An Interview with Jane Yolen," *The Writer* 110, no. 3 (March 1997), 20–21.

103 Jessica Higgs, "Passager," *Emergency Librarian* 25, no. 5, 41.

104 Michelle West, "Armageddon Summer/ The Cure/ Clockwork/ Never Trust a Dead Man," *Fantasy & Science Fiction* 97, no. 2, (August 1999), 45.

105 Jane Yolen and Bruce Coville, "Two Brains, One Book: Or How We Found Our Way to the End of the World," 56.

106 Ibid., 56–57.

107 Jane Yolen, *All Those Secrets of the World* (New York: Little, Brown and Company, 1991), 28.

108 Review of *All Those Secrets of the World, Publishers Weekly* (March 22, 1991), 88.

109 Jane Yolen, *Miz Berlin Walks* (New York: Philomel Books, 1997), 3.

110 Jane Yolen Official Web Site, Jane Yolen's Picture Books: *And Twelve Chinese Acrobats. www.janeyolen.com/blurbs/ andtca2.html.*

111 Carol Otis Hurst, "Review of Granddad Bill's Song," *Teaching Pre K-8* 25, no. 1 (August 1993), 134.

112 Jane Yolen, *A Letter from Phoenix Farm,* 12.

113 Heidi E.Y. Stemple Web Site, Heidi E.Y. Stemple Biography. *www.heidistemple.com/heidibio .html.*

114 Ann G. Brouse, "The Mary Celeste: An Unsolved Mystery from History," *School Library Journal* 45, no. 11 (November 1999), 133.

115 Heidi E.Y. Stemple Web Site, Heidi E.Y. Stemple Books: *The Mary Celeste. www.heidistemple .com/blurbs/maryc.html.*

116 Quoted in Alan Hedblad, ed. "Jane Yolen: Autobiography Feature." *Something About the Author* vol. 111, 216.

117 Jane Yolen and Heidi E.Y. Stemple. *Mirror, Mirror: Forty Folktales for Mothers and Daughters to Share,* xxiii.

118 Quoted in Alan Hedblad, ed. "Jane Yolen: Autobiography Feature." *Something About the Author* vol. 111, 218.

119 Ann St. John, review of *Queen's Own Fool, Horn Book Magazine* 76, no. 3 (May/June 2000), 324.

120 Anita L. Burkam, review of *Girl in a Cage, Horn Book Magazine* 79, no. 1 (Jan/Feb 2003), 86–87.

121 Anita L. Burkam, review of *Prince Across the Water, Horn Book Magazine* 80, no. 6 (Nov/Dec 2004), 720.

122 Kay Weisman, *The Wizard's Map, Booklist* 95, no. 18 (May 15, 1999), 1691.

123 Alice B. McGinty, *Meet Jane Yolen* (New York: Rosen Publishing Group, 2003), 22.

124 Scholastic.com, AuthorsandBooks: Author Booklist, "Jane Yolen's Interview+transcript."

125 Ibid.

126 Jane Yolen, Billie Judy, and Jonathan Stratman. *The Children's Writer at Work Featuring Jane Yolen.*

127 Jane Yolen, *A Letter from Phoenix Farm*, 16.

128 Booksense.com, "How the Book *How Do Dinosaurs Say Goodnight?* Came to be Written," *www.booksense.com/people/ archive/yolenjane.jsp.*

129 Stephanie Zvirin, review of *How Do Dinosaurs Say Goodnight? Booklist* 96, no. 15 (April 1, 2000), 1456.

130 DownHomeBooks.com, Author Interviews: January 2004 Jane Yolen.

131 Jane Yolen Official Web Site, Jane Yolen's Picture Books: *Harvest Home. www.janeyolen .com/blurbs/harvesth.html.*

132 Jane Yolen Official Web Site, Jane Yolen's Picture Books: *Off We Go! www.janeyolen .com/blurbs/offweg2.html.*

133 Susan Scheps, review of *Off We Go! School Library Journal* 46, no. 5 (May 2000), 159.

134 Jane Yolen Official Web Site, Jane Yolen's Picture Books: *Firebird. www.janeyolen .com/blurbs/firebird2.html.*

135 Jane Yolen Official Web Site, Jane Yolen's Picture Books: *Not One Damsel in Distress. www.janey-olen.com/blurbs/ notonedid2.html.*

136 Jane Yolen Official Web Site, Jane Yolen's Picture Books: *Mightier Than the Sword. www.janeyolen.com/blurbs /mightiertts2.html.*

137 Diane Roback, Jennifer M. Brown, and Jason Britton, "Odysseus in the Serpent Maze," *Publishers Weekly* 248, no. 8 (February 19, 2001), 91.

138 Susanna Daniel, *Jane Yolen. The Library of Author Biographies*, 75.

139 Carolyn Carpan's email with Jane Yolen, December 28, 2004.

140 Heidi E.Y. Stemple Web Site, Heidi E.Y. Stemple Biography.

141 Heidi E.Y. Stemple Web Site, Frequently Asked Questions. *www.heidistemple.com/faqs.html.*

142 Jane Yolen and Heidi E.Y. Stemple. *Mirror, Mirror: Forty Folktales for Mothers and Daughters to Share*, xx.

143 Carolyn Carpan's email with Jane Yolen, December 28, 2004.

144 Scholastic.com, AuthorsandBooks: Author Booklist, "Jane Yolen's Interview+transcript."

145 Jane Yolen, Billie Judy, and Jonathan Stratman, *The Children's Writer at Work Featuring Jane Yolen*.

146 Ibid.

147 Quoted in Alan Hedblad, ed. "Jane Yolen: Autobiography Feature." *Something About the Author* vol. 111, 220.

1939 Jane Hyatt Yolen born February 11, in New York City, New York.

1940 The Yolen family moves to California.

1942 The Yolen family moves back to New York City. Brother Steven Hyatt Yolen born November 4.

1944 Father, Will Yolen, goes to England to serve in World War II. Yolen lives with her mother, Isabelle (Berlin) Yolen, brother Steven, and her Berlin grandparents in Virginia.

1945 The Yolen family returns to New York City.

1952 The Yolen family moves to Westport, Connecticut.

1956 Graduates from Staples High School in Westport.

1960 Graduates with a bachelor of arts degree from Smith College. Works as a production assistant at *Saturday Review* magazine.

1961 Sells first book, *Pirates in Petticoats*, on her birthday. Works as an assistant editor at Gold Medal Books.

1962 Marries David W. Stemple on September 2. Works as an associate editor at Rutledge Press.

1963 Works as an assistant juvenile editor at Alfred A. Knopf, Inc. *Pirates in Petticoats* published.

1964 *The Witch Who Wasn't* published.

1965 Travels with David around Europe, Israel, and Greece.

1966 Returns to the United States. David accepts job at University of Massachusetts Computer Center. Daughter Heidi Elisabet Stemple born July 1.

1967 *The Emperor and the Kite* published.

1968 Son Adam Douglas Stemple born April 30.

1969 Move to Bolton, Massachusetts.

1970 Son Jason Frederic Stemple born May 21. Isabelle dies.

1971 Joins Religious Society of Friends (Quakers). Move to Phoenix Farm in Hatfield, Massachusetts.

1974 Joins board of directors of Society of Children's Book Writers. Publishes *The Girl Who Cried Flowers and Other Tales* and *The Boy Who Had Wings*.

1975 Begins Ph.D. program in Children's Literature at University of Massachusetts. Publishes *The Transfigured Hart*.

1976 Graduates from the University of Massachusetts with a master of education degree.

1977 Becomes a member of board of directors at the Children's Literature Association. *The Seeing Stick* published.

1980 Publishes first book in Commander Toad series, *Commander Toad in Space.*

1981 Publishes *The Gift of Sarah Barker.*

1982 Will moves in with Yolen and her family at Phoenix Farm.

1985 Will dies.

1986 Begins two-year term as president of Science Fiction Writers of America. *Favorite Folk Tales from Around the World* published.

1987 Publishes *Owl Moon.*

1988 *Owl Moon* wins Caldecott Medal. *The Devil's Arithmetic* published; wins Nebula Award. Edits imprint *Jane Yolen Books* for Harcourt Brace Jovanovich.

1991 Publishes autobiographical *All Those Secrets of the World.*

1994 Yolen and David buy half-interest in Wayside in St. Andrews, Scotland; begin spending summers at Wayside.

1995 Granddaughter Maddison Jane Piatt born.

1996 Publishes *Passager* and *Hobby.*

1997 Publishes *Merlin* and *Miz Berlin Walks*. Daughter Heidi and her husband take Glendon Alexandria Callan-Piatt into their home.

1998 Granddaughter Alison Isabelle born. Publishes *Armageddon Summer* with coauthor Bruce Coville.

2000 Publishes first book in Dinosaurs series, *How Do Dinosaurs Say Good Night?* Launches website "The Book on Jane Yolen." Glendon Alexandria Callan-Piatt is adopted into the Stemple family.

2002 Grandson David Francis born. David treated for inoperable brain tumor.

2003 Twin granddaughters Caroline Lee and Amelia Hyatt born.

2004 Begins on-line journal on website.

THE DEVIL'S ARITHMETIC

In this controversial young adult novel, 12-year-old Hannah Stern time travels to Poland during the Holocaust. The Nazis capture her and she is sent to a concentration camp, where she meets Rivka. Rivka teaches Hannah to fight against the terrible conditions in the camps and tells her she must survive to tell the story of the Holocaust. Instead, Hannah takes Rivka's place when she is chosen for the gas chamber. As Hannah enters the gas chamber, she returns home to her family's Passover service.

HOW DO DINOSAURS SAY GOOD NIGHT?

In *How Do Dinosaurs Say Good Night?* many different kinds of dinosaurs learn how to go to bed without complaining to their human parents. The names of the different kinds of dinosaurs can be found on the pages although they are hidden on the bed, the wall, or the bedroom floor. Readers will also enjoy *How Do Dinosaurs Get Well Soon?*, *How Do Dinosaurs Clean Their Rooms?*, and *How Do Dinosaurs Count to Ten?*

OWL MOON

Owl Moon features a father and daughter, based on Yolen's husband David and daughter Heidi, who go searching for an owl in the woods on a dark winter night. The anonymous child describes her excitement and anticipation. But her brothers have told her when you go owling, you may not always see an owl. Finally, Pa and his daughter are rewarded with an answering call from a beautiful owl and return home satisfied.

1963 *Pirates in Petticoats, See This Little Line*

1964 *The Witch Who Wasn't*

1965 *Gwinellen, the Princess Who Could Not Sleep*

1966 *Trust a City Kid* (with Anne Huston)

1967 *The Emperor and the Kite, The Minstrel and the Mountain, Isabel's Noel*

1968 *Greyling: A Picture Story from the Islands of Shetland, World on a String: The Story of Kites, The Longest Name on the Block*

1969 *The Wizard of Washington Square, The Inway Investigators: or, the Mystery at McCracken Place*

1970 *It All Depends, Hobo Toad and the Motorcycle Gang, The Seventh Mandarin*

1971 *The Bird of Time*

1972 *The Girl Who Loved the Wind, Friend: The Story of George Fox and the Quakers, The Fireside Song Book of Birds and Beasts* (with Barbara Green)

1973 *The Wizard Islands, Zoo 2000: Twelve Stories of Science Fiction and Fantasy Beasts*

1974 *Ring Out! A Book of Bells, The Girl Who Cried Flowers and Other Tales, The Boy Who Had Wings, The Adventures of Eeka Mouse, The Rainbow Rider, The Magic Three of Solatia*

1975 *The Little Spotted Fish, The Transfigured Hart*

1976 *Milkweed Days, The Moon Ribbon and Other Tales, Simple Gifts: The Story of the Shakers, An Invitation to the Butterfly Ball*

1977 *The Seeing Stick, The Sultan's Perfect Tree, The Hundredth Dove and Other Tales, Hannah Dreaming, The Lady and the Merman, Rounds About Rounds* (with Barbara Green), *The Giants' Farm* [Giants Series]

1978 *Spider Jane, The Simple Prince, No Bath Tonight, The Mermaid's Three Wisdoms, Shape Shifters*

1979 *Dream Weaver and Other Tales, The Giants Go Camping* [Giants Series], *All in the Woodland Early: An ABC Book*

1980 *Spider Jane on the Move, Mice on Ice, Commander Toad in Space* [Commander Toad Series], *The Robot and Rebecca: The Mystery of the Code-Carrying Kids* [Robot and Rebecca Series], *How Beastly! A Menagerie of Nonsense Poems, Dragon Night and Other Lullabies*

1981 *Shirlick Holmes and the Case of the Wandering Wardrobe, The Acorn Quest, Brothers of the Wind, Sleeping Ugly, The Boy Who Spoke Chimp, Uncle Lemon's Spring, The Robot and Rebecca and the Missing Owser* [Robot and Rebecca Series], *The Gift of Sarah Barker*

1982 *Commander Toad and the Planet of the Grapes* [Commander Toad Series], *Neptune Rising: Songs and Tales of the Undersea Folk, Dragon's Blood* [Pit Dragon Trilogy]

1983 *Commander Toad and the Big Black Hole* [Commander Toad Series]

1984 *The Stone Silenus, Children of the Wolf, Heart's Blood* [Pit Dragon Trilogy]

1985 *Commander Toad and the Dis-Asteroid* [Commander Toad Series]

1986 *The Sleeping Beauty, Commander Toad and the Intergalactic Spy* [Commander Toad Series], *The Lullaby Songbook* (with Adam Stemple), *Ring of Earth: A Child's Book of Seasons, Dragons and Dreams* (with Martin H. Greenberg and Charles G. Waugh)

1987 *Owl Moon, A Sending of Dragons* [Pit Dragon Trilogy], *Commander Toad and the Space Pirates* [Commander Toad Series], *The Three Bears Rhyme Book, Spaceships and Spells* (with Martin H. Greenberg and Charles G. Waugh), *Piggins* [Piggins Series]

1988 *Picnic with Piggins* [Piggins Series], *Piggins and the Royal Wedding* [Piggins Series], *The Devil's Arithmetic, Werewolves: A Collection of Original Stories* (with Martin H. Greenberg)

1989 *Dove Isabeau, The Lap-Time Song and Play Book* (with Adam Stemple), *Best Witches: Poems for Halloween, The Faery Flag: Stories and Poems of Fantasy and the Supernatural, Things That Go Bump in the Night* (with Martin H. Greenberg)

1990 *Baby Bear's Bedtime Book, Sky Dogs, Tam Lin: An Old Ballad, Elfabet: An ABC of Elves, Letting Swift River Go, The Dragon's Boy, Bird Watch, Dinosaur Dances, 2041 AD: Twelve Stories about the Future by Top Science Fiction Writers*

1991 *Vampires* (with Martin H. Greenberg), *Wizard's Hall, Hark! A Christmas Sampler, Wings, All Those Secrets of the World*

1992 *Encounter, Eeny, Meeny, Miney Mole, A Letter from Phoenix Farm, Street Rhymes Around the World, Jane Yolen's Mother Goose Songbook*

1993 *Mouse's Birthday, Hands, Honkers, Travelers Rose, Weather Report, Raining Cats and Dogs, What Rhymes with Moon, Here There Be Dragons*

1994 *Jane Yolen's Songs of Summer, Beneath the Ghost Moon, Grandad Bill's Song, And Twelve Chinese Acrobats, Good Griselle, The Girl in the Golden Bower, Old Dame Counterpane, Little Mouse and Elephant: A Tale from Turkey, The Musicians of Bremen: A Tale From Germany, Alphabestiary: Animal Poems from A to Z, Sacred Places, Animal Fare: Zoological Nonsense Poems, Jane Yolen's Old MacDonald Song Book* (with Adam Stemple), *Here There Be Unicorns*

1995 *The Ballad of the Pirate Queens, Before the Storm, A Sip of Aesop, Merlin and the Dragons, The Wild Hunt, The Three Bears Holiday Rhyme Book, Water Music: Poems for Children, Here There Be Witches, Camelot: A Collection of Original Arthurian Tales, The Haunted House: A Collection of Original Stories* (with Martin H. Greenberg)

1996 *Meet the Monsters* (with Heidi E.Y. Stemple), *Sing Noel* (with Adam Stemple), *Milk and Honey: A Year of Jewish Holidays* (with Adam Stemple), *Welcome to the Sea of Sand, Mother Earth, Father Sky: Poems of Our Planet, O Jerusalem, Sea Watch: A Book of Poetry, Sky Scrape/City Scape: Poems of City Life, Passager* [Young Merlin Trilogy], *Hobby* [Young Merlin Trilogy], *Here There Be Angels*

1997 *Merlin* [Young Merlin Trilogy], *Nocturne, Child of Faerie, Child of Earth, Miz Berlin Walks, Once Upon a Bedtime Story: Classic Tales, The Sea Man, Twelve Impossible Things Before Breakfast, Once Upon Ice and Other Frozen Poems*

1998 *Welcome to the Ice House, Tea with an Old Dragon: A Story of Sophia Smith, Founder of Smith College, House, House, King Long Shanks, Pegasus the Flying Horse, The Book of Fairy Holidays, Raising Yoder's Barn, Prince of Egypt, The Liars' Book, Commander Toad and the Voyage Home* [Commander Toad Series], *The Wizard's Map* [Tartan Magic Series], *Snow, Snow: Winter Poems for Children, The Originals: Animals That Time Forgot, Here There Be Ghosts, Armageddon Summer* (with Bruce Coville)

1999 *Mary Celeste: An Unsolved Mystery from History* (with Heidi E.Y. Stemple), *Moonball, The Pictish Child* [Tartan Magic Series]

2000 *How Do Dinosaurs Say Good Night?*, *Off We Go!*, *Harvest Home*, *Where Have the Unicorns Gone?*, *Welcome to the River Grass*, *The Wolf Girls: An Unsolved Mystery from History*, *Color Me a Rhyme: Nature Poems for Young People*, *Not One Damsel in Distress: World Folktales for Strong Girls*, *Boots and the Seven Leaguers: A Rock-and-Troll Novel*, *Sherwood: A Collection of Original Robin Hood Stories*, *Mirror, Mirror: Forty Folktales for Mothers and Daughters to Share*.

2001 *The Hurrying Child*, *Dear Mother, Dear Daughter: Poems for Young People* (with Heidi E.Y. Stemple), *Odysseus in the Serpent Maze* (with Robert J. Harris) [Young Heroes Series], *Queen's Own Fool* (with Robert J. Harris) [Stuart Quartet]

2002 *Firebird*, *The Bagpiper's Ghost* [Tartan Magic Series], *Girl in Cage* (with Robert J. Harris) [Stuart Quartet], *Time for Naps*, *Animal Train*, *Bedtime for Bunny: A Book to Touch and Feel*, *Wild Wings: Poems for Young People*, *Horizons: Poems As Far As the Eye Can See*, *Hippolyta and the Curse of the Amazons* (with Robert J. Harris) [Young Heroes Series]

2003 *The Sea King*, *My Brothers' Flying Machine: Wilbur, Orville, and Me*, *How Do Dinosaurs Get Well Soon?*, *Roanoke, The Lost Colony: An Unsolved Mystery from History* (with Heidi E.Y. Stemple), *Hoptoad*, *The Flying Witch*, *Least Things: Poems About Small Natures*, *Sword of the Rightful King: A Novel of King Arthur*, *Mightier Than the Sword: World Folktales for Strong Boys*, *Atalanta and the Arcadian Beast* (with Robert J. Harris) [Young Heroes Series]

2004 *How Do Dinosaurs Count to Ten?*, *How Do Dinosaurs Clean Their Rooms?*, *Salem Witch Trials: An Unsolved Mystery from History* (with Heidi E.Y. Stemple), *The Barefoot Book of Ballet Stories* (with Heidi E.Y. Stemple), *Fine Feathered Friends*, *Jason and the Gorgon's Blood* (with Robert J. Harris) [Young Heroes Series], *Prince Across the Water* (with Robert J. Harris) [Stuart Quartet]

2005 *The Perfect Wizard: Hans Christian Andersen*, *Grandma's Hurrying Child*

Jane Yolen has created many memorable characters. Some of them, like the young child in *Owl Moon* and the many dinosaurs in Yolen's How Do Dinosaurs series, are without names. The unnamed child in *Owl Moon* is actually a girl, based on Yolen's daughter Heidi.

HANNAH STERN is a 12-year-old Jewish girl who time-travels to Poland during the Holocaust. Hannah is captured by the Nazis. She is sent to a concentration camp, where she meets Rivka. Rivka teaches Hannah to fight against the terrible conditions in the camps and tells her she must survive to tell the story of the Holocaust. Instead, Hannah takes Rivka's place when she is chosen for the gas chamber. As Hannah enters the gas chamber, she returns home to her family's Passover service. Actress Kirsten Dunst portrayed Hannah in the movie version of *The Devil's Arithmetic.*

JAKKIN STEWART, a 15-year-old servant in Master Sarkkhan's dragon barns, steals a dragon hatchling. In the first book of the Pit Dragon trilogy, *Dragon's Blood*, Jakkin trains the dragon, named Heart's Blood, to be a great fighter. In *Heart's Blood*, the next book in the series, Jakkin is the new Dragon Master. Jakkin must rescue Akki, the woman he loves. Jakkin and Akki save Heart's Blood's baby dragons after she dies in battle. In *A Sending of Dragons* Jakkin must protect the baby dragons from capture. Jakkin is eventually able to end feudalism and slavery on Austar IV.

1968 *The Emperor and the Kite* wins Lewis Carroll Shelf Award and Caldecott Medal Honors.

1974 *The Girl Who Cried Flowers and Other Tales* wins Golden Kite Award.

1975 *The Transfigured Hart* wins Golden Kite Honors.

1976 *Moon Ribbon and Other Tales* wins Golden Kite Honors.

1977 *The Seeing Stick* wins Christopher Medal.

1987 *Favorite Folk Tales from Around the World* wins World Fantasy Award.

1988 *Owl Moon* wins Caldecott Medal. Wins Kerlan Award for achievement in children's literature.

1989 *The Devil's Arithmetic* wins the Jewish Book Council Award and Association of Jewish Libraries Sydney Taylor Book Award.

1992 Yolen wins Regina Medal for body of writing in children's literature.

1993 *Briar Rose* wins Mythopoeic Fantasy Award.

1998 The Young Merlin trilogy *(Passager/Hobby/Merlin)* wins Mythopoeic Fantasy Award.

1999 Yolen wins Remarkable Women Award from Smith College.

2000 *How Do Dinosaurs Say Good Night?* wins Christopher Medal.

2001 *Armageddon Summer* wins California Young Reader Medal.

2002 *Wild Wings* wins National Outdoor Book Awards.

2003 Yolen wins National Storytelling Network 2003 ORACLE Award for outstanding contributions to the literary body of storytelling.

2003 Yolen awarded Honorary Doctorate from Smith College.

Daniel, Susanna. *Jane Yolen. The Library of Author Biographies.* New York: Rosen Publishing Group, 2004.

Hedblad, Alan, ed. "Jane Yolen: Autobiography Feature." *Something About the Author*, vol. 111. Detroit, MI: Gale Group, 2000.

McGinty, Alice B. *Meet Jane Yolen*. About the Author. New York: Rosen Publishing Group, 2003.

Watson, Tracey, ed. "Jane Hyatt Yolen," *Contemporary Authors: New Revision Series* vol. 126. Detroit, MI: Gale Research, Inc., 2004.

Yolen, Jane. Jane Yolen Official Web Site. *www.janeyolen.com.*

———. *A Letter from Phoenix Farm.* Katonah, NY: Richard C. Owen Publishers, Inc., 1992.

Yolen, Jane, Billie Judy, and Jonathan Stratman. *The Children's Writer at Work Featuring Jane Yolen*. VHS. Bainbridge Island, WA: Reel Life Productions, 1997.

Yolen, Jane, and Heidi E.Y. Stemple. *Mirror, Mirror: Forty Folktales for Mothers and Daughters to Share*. New York: Viking, 2000.

Sacco, Margaret T. "Jane Yolen." *Writers for Young Adults*, Ted Hipple, ed. New York: Charles Scribner's Sons, 1997, 409–420.

www.janeyolen.com

> *[Jane Yolen Official Web Site. Visitors to Yolen's website can find information about her books and the many awards her books have won. Biographical information includes many photos of Yolen at various stages of her life. There are also pictures of Yolen with her friends, family, and colleagues. Fans can also find her travel schedule, which includes Yolen's public appearances at conferences, bookstores, and other events. There is a list of frequently asked questions for kids and a list of resources for teachers. Yolen also provides information for other writers. There is also a "What's New" section and Yolen's on-line journal.]*

CAROLYN CARPAN is an Assistant Professor and Reference Librarian at Rollins College in Winter Park, Florida. She holds a master's degree in Library and Information Studies from Dalhousie University in Halifax, Nova Scotia, and a master's degree in Women's Studies from the Memorial University of Newfoundland in St. John's, Newfoundland. She is the author of the book *Rocked by Romance: A Guide to Teen Romance Fiction* (Libraries Unlimited, 2004).